APPOINTING CENTRAL BANKERS

THE POLITICS OF MONETARY POLICY IN THE UNITED STATES AND THE EUROPEAN MONETARY UNION

This book examines how the president and the Senate influence monetary policy by appointing Federal Reserve members. The book answers three questions about the appointment process and its effects. First, do politicians influence monetary policy through Federal Reserve appointments? Second, who influences the process – the president alone or both the president and the Senate? Third, what explains the structure of the Federal Reserve appointment process?

The analysis shows the conditions under which the president alone, both the president and the Senate, or neither may influence monetary policy with Federal Reserve appointments. The structure of the process reflects historical political battles between the Democrats and Republicans regarding the centralization of authority to set monetary policy within the Federal Reserve System.

The study extends the analysis to the European Central Bank and shows that the Federal Reserve process is more representative of society than the European Central Bank process.

Kelly H. Chang is currently the Chief Currency and Political Strategist at UBS Private Banking. Prior to her current position, she was an Assistant Professor of Political Science and Public Affairs at the University of Wisconsin-Madison and a Robert Wood Johnson Scholar in Health Policy at the University of Michigan. While holding a National Science Foundation Graduate Research Fellowship, she received a Ph.D. and M.A. in political science and M.A. in economics from Stanford University. She has written and published a number of articles on political economy centering around central banks and political appointments.

POLITICAL ECONOMY OF INSTITUTIONS AND DECISIONS

Series Editors

Randall Calvert, Washington University, St. Louis
Thrainn Eggertsson, Max Planck Institute, Germany, and University of Iceland

Founding Editors

James E. Alt, Harvard University
Douglass C. North, Washington University, St. Louis

Other Books in the Series

Alberto Alesina and Howard Rosenthal, *Partisan Politics, Divided Government, and the Economy*
Lee J. Alston, Thrainn Eggertsson, and Douglass C. North, eds., *Empirical Studies in Institutional Change*
Lee J. Alston and Joseph P. Ferrie, *Southern Paternalism and the Rise of the American Welfare State: Economics, Politics, and Institutions, 1865–1965*
James E. Alt and Kenneth Shepsle, eds., *Perspectives on Positive Political Economy*
Jeffrey S. Banks and Eric A. Hanushek, eds., *Modern Political Economy: Old Topics, New Directions*
Yoram Barzel, *Economic Analysis of Property Rights*, 2nd edition
Robert Bates, *Beyond the Miracle of the Market: The Political Economy of Agrarian Development in Kenya*
Peter Cowhey and Mathew McCubbins, eds., *Structure and Policy in Japan and the United States*
Gary W. Cox, *The Efficient Secret: The Cabinet and the Development of Political Parties in Victorian England*
Gary W. Cox, *Making Votes Count: Strategic Coordination in the World's Electoral System*
Jean Ensminger, *Making a Market: The Institutional Transformation of an African Society*
David Epstein and Sharyn O'Halloran, *Delegating Powers: A Transaction Cost Politics Approach to Policy Making under Separate Powers*
Kathryn Firmin-Sellers, *The Transformation of Property Rights in the Gold Coast: An Empirical Analysis Applying Rational Choice Theory*
Clark C. Gibson, *Politics and Poachers: The Political Economy of Wildlife Policy in Africa*
Ron Harris, *The Legal Framework of Business Organization: England, 1720–1844*

Continued on page following index

APPOINTING
CENTRAL BANKERS

*The Politics of Monetary Policy in the United States
and the European Monetary Union*

KELLY H. CHANG

CAMBRIDGE
UNIVERSITY PRESS

PUBLISHED BY THE PRESS SYNDICATE OF THE UNIVERSITY OF CAMBRIDGE
The Pitt Building, Trumpington Street, Cambridge, United Kingdom

CAMBRIDGE UNIVERSITY PRESS
The Edinburgh Building, Cambridge CB2 2RU, UK
40 West 20th Street, New York, NY 10011-4211, USA
477 Williamstown Road, Port Melbourne, VIC 3207, Australia
Ruiz de Alarcón 13, 28014 Madrid, Spain
Dock House, The Waterfront, Cape Town 8001, South Africa

http://www.cambridge.org

First published 2003

Printed in the United States of America

Typeface Sabon 10/13 pt.   *System* LATEX 2$_\varepsilon$ [TB]

A catalog record for this book is available from the British Library.

Library of Congress Cataloging in Publication data available

ISBN 0 521 82333 1 hardback

Contents

Contents

Contents

List of Figures

List of Tables

Acknowledgments

This book is based on my doctoral dissertation, "Their People = Their Policy: The President, Congress, and Appointments to the Federal Reserve." It is impossible to thank everyone who helped me over the years from the dissertation stage through the book process, but here's an attempt.

At Cambridge, Randy Calvert, the series editor, deserves an enormous amount of credit for suffering through several versions of the manuscript and always providing me with thoughtful and insightful comments. His comments, along with those of two anonymous referees, transformed the manuscript from a dissertation to the book as it stands today. The manuscript improved significantly through this process. I would also like to thank Lew Bateman, the political science editor, for supporting the manuscript and for patiently answering my many questions.

At Stanford University, my committee members deserve special credit. I am especially indebted to my principal advisor, Barry Weingast, for his patience and honesty. Despite his impossibly busy schedule as the Department Chair, Barry always made time to comment on a paper or to advise me on my career plans. I am also greatly indebted to Doug Rivers, who provided invaluable advice and help on the empirical sections in addition to his excellent suggestions on technical writing. I have also benefited greatly from John Ferejohn's encouragement, interest, and last but not least, his Pizza and Politics seminar series which must have one of the world's toughest crowds. Speaking of tough crowds, Terry Moe's willingness to carefully and frankly criticize the main arguments crucially helped to improve the work. Roger Noll, my oral defense chair, also provided important comments on everything – for example, the formal models, the empirical analysis, and the presentation of the work.

I would like to thank Heather and Susan Havrilesky and Ed Tower at Duke University for help in obtaining Thomas Havrilesky's SAFER dataset of presidential signaling. Thanks also to Rudy Espino, Sarah Keim, and Doug Long, who provided careful and painstaking research assistance.

I am also grateful to the following people for their help and support: Oliver Adler, Norma Alvarez, Mike Bailey, Matt Bartels, Heather Basarab, Jenna Bednar, Erik Berglof, Dina Boomla, Lawrence Broz, Maria Cancian, Brandice Canes-Wrone, David Canon, Julie Cullen, Rui de Figueiredo, Charles Franklin, Rob Franzese, Bruno Frey, Geoff Garrett, Kurt Gaubatz, Ed Green, Michael Herron, Dan Kelemen, Laurie Koloski, Myong Lee, Dave Leheny, Dave Lewis, Bart Lipman, Tani Maher, Nolan McCarty, Irwin Morris, Peter Moser, Scott Page, Jonathan Parker, Andy Rutten, Larry Samuelson, Bill Sandholm, Anne Sartori, Heiner Schulz, Chuck Shipan, Ken Shotts, Ravi Singh, the Stanford Cycling Club (too many to mention individually), John Taylor, Shawn Treier, Isabelle Vautravers, Craig Volden, Chris Way, Scott Wilson, and Alan Wiseman. I would also like to thank the many seminar participants over the years.

I would finally like to acknowledge financial support from the following institutions: the Federal Reserve Bank of Minneapolis, the National Science Foundation, the Robert Wood Johnson Foundation, UBS AG, the University of Michigan, and the University of Wisconsin-Madison. At the University of Wisconsin, Dave Trubek at the European Union Center and Don Nichols at World Affairs and the Global Economy deserve special mention for their financial support of the European Monetary Union portion of this book.

I

Introduction

Central banks are often independent, but the degree of independence varies among the banks and over time. Until recently, the British government dictated the Bank of England's monetary policy (Schaling 1995: 91–2). In contrast, the Deutsche Bundesbank controlled policy without government interference (Schaling 1995: 95–6).[1] De Nederlandsche Bank straddled the two extremes; in the event of disagreement, the Dutch finance minister and the central bank had to compromise (Schaling 1995: 93–4). Both the Bundesbank and De Nederlandsche Bank are now parts of the European System of Central Banks, and both should be more similar in their independence; the statute for the new system explicitly prohibits any central bank from taking government instructions (Grilli, Masciandro, and Tabellini 1991; see Cukierman 1992 and Schaling 1995 for excellent reviews of the existing indices of central bank independence).

Although central banks vary in independence, most share a common characteristic: political appointments. Despite the safeguards of central bank independence – for example, no government instructions or closed policy meetings – politicians appoint monetary policy makers. Thus, appointments remain a potential avenue of political influence on monetary policy. The idea behind appointments is simple: if a politician appoints someone like herself, then the appointee should act like the politician when setting monetary policy.

However, influence rarely works so directly or easily. The extent to which politicians influence monetary policy through appointments depends on the appointment process itself, particularly two features of the process. First, different branches of government often share the power to

---

[1] Prior to the start of EMU. In January of 1999, the ECB took over the monetary policy setting authority of the Deutsche Bundesbank and De Nederlandsche Bank.

appoint. For some central banks, the cabinet appoints candidates subject to legislative approval (e.g., Japan; Bank of Japan Law, Art 23, ¶1–2). For others, the process is reversed: the legislature or cabinet nominates, and the president appoints (e.g., Germany; European Commission 1998: 40, fn. 3). In either set of cases, those who nominate have first-mover advantage and can have relatively more power in the process.

Second, central banks usually have decision-making boards with multiple members. As a result, politicians can rarely influence policy dramatically with one appointment; they usually have the existing members to contend with. In Sweden, until 1999, this problem did not exist as virtually all terms expired every four years right after each parliamentary election (Schaling 1995: 90–1). In Germany, however, each term lasted eight years, and the terms were staggered over several years.[2] Thus in Sweden, one round of appointments was sufficient to significantly influence policy, while in Germany it was probably not enough.

In short, politicians have to work within the constraints of the process in order to influence monetary policy through appointments. Furthermore, in every country, the appointment process reflects the degree to which the powers are separated or shared in the governmental system. In Sweden, the legislature dominates the process, but legislative dominance does not mean much in the context of unified government; in such a system, both legislative and cabinet approval of nominees would be redundant. In Germany, the legislature nominates, and the executive appoints, and the separation of these powers does make sense because the government is not necessarily unified; the majority party of both the lower house, the Bundestag, and the upper house, the Bundesrat, can differ from that of the president.

In the United States, as in Germany, the appointment power is also shared between the executive and legislative branches. In accordance with Article II, Section 2 of the U.S. Constitution,[3] the president appoints Federal Reserve (Fed) members with the advice and consent of the Senate. The president has first-mover advantage in his powers to nominate, but his choice must be conditioned by the Senate's preferences, because of the

---

[2] These features still exist although the Bundesbank no longer sets monetary policy.

[3] "[The President] shall nominate and by and with the advice and consent of the Senate, shall appoint Ambassadors, other public Ministers and Consuls, Judges of the Supreme Court, and all other officers of the United States, whose appointments are not herein otherwise provided for, and which shall be established by law: but the Congress may by law vest the appointment of such inferior officers, as they think proper, in the President alone, in the courts of law, or in the heads of departments."

Senate's power to veto the president's choice. This simple bargaining process, the same process for thousands of federal appointments, produces the policy makers to one of the most powerful institutions in the world – the Federal Reserve. But this particular process, the process for the Fed, has seldom been studied.

This book examines the Fed appointment process and its impact on monetary policy. Because the appointment process repeats in a stable context, it provides an excellent opportunity to examine interbranch bargaining in an area rarely studied by economists – appointment politics – and in a policy subject rarely studied by political scientists – monetary policy. What is the appointment process? How does it really work? Which politicians influence appointments? Who designed the process and for what purpose? This book attempts to tackle these questions with a detailed theoretical and empirical study of Fed appointments that is extended to the new European Central Bank (ECB) – often called the world's most independent central bank.

1.1 THE BOOK'S MAIN QUESTIONS

In mid-January of 1996, Alan Blinder, the Vice Chairman of the Federal Reserve, announced his imminent resignation. Two days later, the Clinton administration expressed interest in the possible nomination of Felix Rohatyn (Wessel 1996: A2), a well-known easy monetary policy advocate. In a vociferous and public attack, Senate Republicans subsequently opposed Rohatyn's candidacy and specifically his potential easy influence on monetary policy (Wilke and Frisby 1996: A3, A16). Rohatyn withdrew within days from consideration although the administration had yet to announce a formal nomination (Wilke 1996b).

About ten days later, the Clinton administration nominated Alice Rivlin, the White House Budget Director, and an academic economist, Laurence Meyer, for an additional vacancy. Both Rivlin and Meyer were widely seen as much more conservative candidates compared to Rohatyn. This time the Senate Republicans were far more receptive. Senator Mack of the Banking Committee remarked that the new members "... are likely to give us a board committed to price stability, and that's what we want to see" (quoted in Wilke 1996a).

This story highlights several important insights into the political appointment process of the American system. First, politicians care about appointments because they believe appointments affect policy. Senator Mack objected to Rohatyn's possible easy influence on monetary policy and supported Rivlin and Meyer's likely contributions to price stability. Second, the Senate as well as the president may influence the appointment process. Rohatyn's withdrawal from candidacy followed heavy Senate criticism. Third, prior to the formal nomination, the president and Senate engage in bargaining regarding the possible nominees. The back and forth between the president and Senate and Rohatyn's withdrawal preceded a formal administration nomination.

But these insights follow from one anecdote. Do they generalize to other appointments – in other American agencies, in other central banks, or in the Fed? This study addresses the question theoretically and empirically with respect to the Fed with an extension to the ECB. More precisely, the study addresses three specific questions. First, do politicians influence monetary policy through appointments? Second, who influences appointments – the president and Senate jointly or just the president? Third, what explains the structure of Fed appointments?

1.2 QUESTION 1: DO POLITICIANS INFLUENCE MONETARY POLICY THROUGH APPOINTMENTS?

It seems reasonable to assume politicians want their monetary policy preferences to be reflected in monetary policy. Monetary policy profoundly influences the economy, and the economy is often the key to electoral success. A strong empirical relationship exists between the economy's performance and voting for the incumbent party (Kramer 1971; Stigler 1973; Tufte 1975; Fair 1978, 1980; Alesina and Rosenthal 1989, 1995; Erikson 1990; Alesina, Londregan, and Rosenthal 1993). For example, Reagan took advantage of this relationship in 1980 with the campaign slogan, "Are you better off than you were four years ago?"

Because politicians know the appointment process and the Fed's structure, they should be able to strategically appoint Fed members in order to obtain their preferred policy. I use this logic to construct a model of how politicians' monetary policy preferences translate to policy, and then empirically test the model's predictions to see if political influence occurs in the manner specified by the model.

In answer to this first question, this book's results indicate that politicians do influence monetary policy with Fed appointments. Despite the Fed's highly regarded independence, appointments remain an important avenue of political influence on monetary policy. In other words, independence does not imply total freedom from political authority. The Fed may have more autonomy compared to other American agencies, and the Fed is more autonomous compared to most central banks, but it hardly runs amok. By appointing the appropriate members, the president and Senate basically keep the Fed in line with their preferences while still allowing for the Fed's freedom on a day-to-day basis.

The question of political influence and monetary policy has received much attention in economics, but the perspective is different from the one adopted in this book. From the economic perspective (see particularly Kydland and Prescott 1977), political influence is a *problem* that needs to be solved. The problem starts with the policy makers' incentive to deviate from the socially optimal inflation rate of zero. If policy makers unexpectedly inflate, unemployment decreases, but because economic agents know that policy makers have these incentives, they expect the policy makers to deviate. Because expectations determine inflation, the outcome is positive inflation, which is suboptimal. In their landmark study, Kydland and Prescott (1977) called this the problem of "time inconsistency."

Subsequent economic studies concentrated on two sets of solutions to the problem of time inconsistency. The first was reputation. Barro and Gordon (1983) found that through repeated interactions, policy makers can convince economic agents of their dedication to zero inflation. The second set focused on institutions. Rogoff (1985) and others examined how delegation of monetary authority to a conservative central banker renders society better off by lowering inflation and increasing output. Subsequent works in central bank independence found that appointment features such as longer terms, timing around elections, and conservative biases of the central bankers are pareto efficient (Frey and Schneider 1981; Grilli, Masciandro, and Tabellini 1991; Lohmann 1992; Waller 1992; Alesina and Summers 1993; Waller and Walsh 1996; see Cukierman 1992; Persson and Tabellini 1994, 1999 for excellent summaries).

The problem of political influence is further complicated by the existence of political parties. The "political business cycles" literature showed how policy can fluctuate suboptimally according to partisan interests (Nordhaus 1975; Hibbs 1977; Rogoff and Sibert 1988; Persson and Tabellini 1990; and Rogoff 1990). In a vein similar to Barro and Gordon, Alesina (1987) demonstrated that if the parties cooperate on setting a credible policy in a repeated, two-party game, the cycles attenuated. Building on Rogoff's institutional solution, Waller (1992) and Waller and Walsh (1996) found that the partisanship of central bankers can be reduced by working with the timing of central bank appointments around elections.

The modeling choices in this literature reflect the interest in solving the problem of political influence. The models are dynamic, general equilibrium representations of the entire economy with few institutional details. The actors are represented by homogenous types or representative agents. For example, one central banker represents all central bankers. In the political business cycle models, the policy makers are divided into two parties, but for each party, one party member represents the entire party. Furthermore, the work is more theoretically than empirically developed.[4] But these choices are understandable because the purpose of these models is to show whether a variation in the setup, the proposed solution, leads to optimal outcomes in economic aggregates such as inflation or output. In such models, details may add unnecessary complications.

A group of economists and political scientists have taken an approach different from the preceding general equilibrium models. The quantitative work is empirical and focuses on the Fed's reaction function: regression models with monetary policy as a dependent variable and political influence measures as independent variables (e.g., Beck 1982a; Chappell, Havrilesky and McGregor 1993, 1995; Havrilesky 1993, 1995; Morris 1994, 2000). In particular, Havrilesky (1993, 1995) used reaction functions extensively to find the influence of the president, Congress, and interest groups. On appointment specifically, the results of Morris (1991, 1994, 2000) and Keech and Morris (1996) support presidential and congressional influence through appointments. Morris' thesis (1994) provided the first efforts to formalize a theory of Fed appointments. There are also some very careful qualitative studies by Woolley (1984), who delved into the political meaning of independence, and Kettl (1986), who focused on the evolution of the Chair's role.

In contrast to the studies in time inconsistency, central bank independence, and political business cycles, the Fed literature is characterized by an almost opposite set of features. First, few models of strategic interaction exist (exceptions are Morris 1994; Morris and Munger 1997), and

---

[4] The empirical work has lagged behind the theoretical breakthroughs. Some evidence suggests a negative relationship between inflation and central bank independence (higher central bank independence implies lower inflation; Grilli, Masciandro, and Tabellini 1991; see Cukierman 1992 for an extensive review). Considerably more empirical work has been done with respect to political business cycles. Starting with Hibbs (1977), the evidence tends to support post-election cycles based on certain conditions predicted by the models (Alesina and Roubini 1990; Persson and Tabellini 1994, 1999). The evidence is not so clear on preelection cycles (Nordhaus 1975; Alesina and Roubini 1990; Persson and Tabellini 1994, 1999).

if they do, the models are static, one-shot games rather than dynamic, repeated games. Second, Fed studies often do make distinctions between different individual actors rather than typologizing them. For example, Chappell, Havrilesky, and McGregor (1993, 1995) examine the differing influences of Reagan and Carter. Third, Fed scholars talk more about the institutions and processes of monetary policy, but there is little formalization of these characteristics. Fourth, in direct contrast to the time inconsistency and central bank independence literature, studies of the Fed are characterized by more empirical than theoretical work.

While both sets of studies provide important findings about central banks, the Fed, and monetary policy, none are quite right for answering the first main question. As this book will show, the appointment process determines how and when influence occurs. The central bank independence literature abstracts from process, as it rightly should, since its concerns are not how the process *actually* works, but rather how central bank relations with politicians *should* work – an essentially normative enterprise, albeit with positive tools. As for the reaction function approach, it is also unsuited to answering the first main question because it seeks to show whether influence exists after any appointment. But not all appointments are alike; influence occurs in certain circumstances but not in others. In this book, those circumstances are clarified through a model of the appointment process that shows that whether influence occurs depends on the direction of policy change desired by the politicians and if the current makeup of the central decision-making board is favorable for moving policy in that direction. Rather than as a *problem* to solve, I treat political influence as a phenomenon about which we want to find out the mechanisms and effects.

1.3 QUESTION 2: WHO INFLUENCES APPOINTMENTS?

Both the president and Senate have distinct powers in the appointment process: the president chooses nominees, but the Senate can veto those nominees. Can the president afford to ignore the Senate, or does the Senate's veto power really mean something?

In fact, the Senate's veto power has substantial bite in the process, as this book will show. The Senate does not have to actually exercise its veto power, and it rarely does; in the case of Fed appointments, the Senate has never rejected a nominee (Morris 2000: 78). The mere threat of the veto is enough to make the president pay attention to the Senate's preferences. If the president does not anticipate the Senate, he faces the consequences – a

7

long, drawn-out confirmation battle that means tolerating whatever policy the current Fed dishes out compared to a possibly better policy if the president compromises with the Senate. For example, rather than fight a war for Rohatyn, the president compromised with his choices of Rivlin and Meyer.

This second question underscores a debate in the political science appointments literature between those who believe the president always anticipates the Senate versus others who believe the president dominates all the time. Proponents of presidential anticipation claim that Senate acquiescence is not Senate powerlessness because the president takes into account the Senate's preferences before formally nominating the candidates (Calvert, McCubbins, and Weingast 1989; Lemieux and Stewart 1990; Hammond and Hill 1993; Morris 1994; Nokken and Sala 2000; Snyder and Weingast 2000). In contrast, presidential dominance scholars claim that the president chooses whomever he pleases, and the Senate will agree because of a norm of deference to the president (Moe 1985, 1987b). Both have used the rarity of Senate rejections as support for their respective theories, but Senate acceptance cannot be used to refute or support either theory: both predict acceptance.[5]

As with many debates, the truth lies somewhere in the middle, as other parts of the bureaucratic delegation literature have concluded. Over the last twenty years, political scientists have gradually modified the principal-agent theory to the realities of the American political setting. Older studies tended to focus on one principal or another, but more recent studies incorporate multiple principals. In the early 80s, the congressional dominance literature examined how Congress influences the bureaucracy through oversight (Weingast and Moran 1983; McCubbins and Schwartz 1984; Weingast 1984). Presidential scholars responded by pointing out the importance of the president through mechanisms such as appointments (Mackenzie 1981; Moe 1985, 1987b). Recent studies take a more holistic approach by considering the president, Congress, the courts, and the bureaucracy together. They show how these institutional actors bargain with one another given their different constitutional powers (Moe 1985, 1987b; McCubbins, Noll, and Weingast 1987; Calvert, McCubbins,

---

[5] The two theories are also observationally equivalent with respect to Senate roll-call votes when: (1) the president's ideal point lies outside the range of the Senate ideal points, and (2) if dominance scholars define Senate deference as median deference rather than unanimous deference. In (1), all senators vote in the same manner regardless of dominance or anticipation. In (2), a majority of the senators vote in the same manner regardless of dominance or anticipation.

and Weingast 1989; Ferejohn and Shipan 1989, 1990; Matthews 1989; Eskridge and Ferejohn 1992; Hammond and Knott 1996; McCarty 1997; Epstein and O'Halloran 1999; Cameron 2000). These studies have identified the conditions under which Congress, the president, or the courts dominate policy and when they truly share powers (see particularly McCarty and Poole 1995; Hammond and Knott 1996).

Those conditions are also apparent in the Fed appointment process. If we start with a model in which the president always anticipates the Senate, there are still cases in which the president clearly dominates, and others in which neither the president nor the Senate dominates. It depends on whether the president and Senate agree on the direction of policy change and on their preferences relative to current monetary policy.

First, if the president and Senate disagree on the direction of policy change, there is deadlock, and they agree to maintain current policy. Any policy change makes one or the other worse off. Clinton faced this situation with his first few appointments to the Fed. Clinton wanted to move policy in an easier direction, but the Republican Senate Banking Committee did not. When he tried to move policy with Rohatyn, the committee objected, and Clinton had to pull Rohatyn's nomination as well as an earlier nomination of Alicia Munnell.

Second, if they agree on the direction of change, but the president likes the current policy more than the Senate, then the president dominates. From the beginning of his first administration, Reagan wanted to move monetary policy in an easier direction. Martha Seger was Reagan's second Fed appointee in 1984. She faced Democratic opposition in the Senate Banking Committee, but the Republican majority in the committee sided with Reagan and wanted policy to ease up even more than Reagan did. With his choice of Seger, Reagan moved policy as far as he could with this one appointment, and the Democratic senators could not stop him.[6]

Third, if they agree on the direction, and the Senate likes the president's preferred policy more than the current policy, then the president again dominates. When Carter appointed Nancy Teeters in 1978, both he and the Senate clearly favored easier policy; the Senate favored less easier policy, but only slightly less. Under these circumstances, Carter was able to choose Teeters who, even today, is pointed out as the quintessential monetary policy liberal.

---

[6] Reagan appointed Seger during a congressional recess and angered the Democrats in the process. The Democrats tried to pass an amendment to withdraw the nomination, but the amendment failed to pass on party lines (Morris 2000: 78).

Finally, if they agree on the direction, but the Senate likes the current policy more than the president does, then the president has to accommodate the Senate. For example, when Reagan appointed Alan Greenspan in 1987, he sought a candidate less hawkish than Paul Volcker. The Senate also wanted someone less hawkish but somewhat more hawkish than Greenspan (Greider 1987: 713–14; Martin 2000: 155–7). But because they agreed that policy should move toward somewhat less vigilance on inflation, and because the President had first-mover advantage in choosing the nominee, Reagan could choose a less hawkish candidate, Greenspan, than the Senate would have preferred. However, he could not have gone further to choose a candidate who was still more liberal without incurring Senate threats of rejection.

These second and third cases therefore show presidential dominance within an anticipation framework. But is there dominance all the time? This book's empirical results indicate that it is unlikely. In a direct comparison of the anticipation and dominance models, anticipation does better most of the time for the Federal Open Market Committee (FOMC) – the Fed's main decision-making body.

In identifying dominance within an anticipation framework, this book fits in with more recent studies of appointments. In their study of Supreme Court appointments, Moraski and Shipan (1999) demonstrate that depending on the policy preferences of the president and Senate relative to the current policy, the president or the Senate or both may influence appointments. Bailey and Chang (1999, 2003) show that in addition to the policy preferences, the costs to each side of further nominations determine whether one, the other, or both the president and Senate influence appointments. McCarty and Razaghian (1999) bring similar concerns to an examination of Senate confirmation times for executive branch appointments.

1.4 QUESTION 3: WHAT EXPLAINS THE STRUCTURE OF FEDERAL RESERVE APPOINTMENTS?

The Federal Reserve Act of 1913 created the Federal Reserve System, which consists of twelve district reserve banks,[7] and two main decision-making institutions in Washington, DC: the Board of Governors (BOG)

---

[7] The twelve district reserve banks are located in New York, Boston, Philadelphia, Richmond, Cleveland, Chicago, Atlanta, Dallas, St. Louis, Minneapolis, Kansas City, and San Francisco.

Table 1.1: *The Structure of the Federal Reserve System*

Institution	Number of Members	Appointment Procedure	Functions
District Reserve Banks	12 banks	Bank presidents – by board of directors with the advice and consent of the BOG	Facilitates payments, supervises and regulates banks, participates on the FOMC
Board of Governors	7	By president with the advice and consent of the Senate	Sets the discount rate, determines reserve requirements, participates on the FOMC
Federal Open Market Committee	12	Composed of 7 BOG members and 5 reserve bank presidents	Primary monetary policy-making body; sets the federal funds rate using open-market operations

and the FOMC (Table 1.1). The FOMC is the principal decision-making body of the Federal Reserve System with primary responsibility for setting monetary policy. In its meetings, which occur approximately every six weeks, the FOMC decides by majority rule whether to change the federal funds rate using *open market operations* – sales and purchases of government securities. The federal funds rate is the rate at which banks lend funds overnight to one another, and it is a crucial determinant of other interest rates such as the prime rate.

The twelve-member FOMC consists of two sets of members. The first is the BOG – seven members in total. By itself, the BOG sets the discount rate, the rate at which the Fed lends funds to banks. The president has the formal power to nominate the BOG members to fourteen-year terms[8] with the advice and consent of the Senate. The Federal Reserve Act provides for two appointments per presidential term, two years apart from one another, but in reality, each of the last five presidents, with the exception of George H.W. Bush (Bush appointed three), has appointed at least four governors per presidential term due to early governors' retirements.

[8] The BOG terms are the longest in federal service with the exception of the life terms for federal court judges.

The president also has the power to appoint both the chairman and vice chairman of the BOG, each of whom has a four-year term and a regular fourteen-year governor's term.

The second set of FOMC members consists of the presidents of the district reserve banks. The twelve reserve banks represent the twelve Federal Reserve districts located throughout the country with disproportionate representation of the eastern seaboard and the midwest. The board of directors of each reserve bank appoints the bank's president with the consent of the BOG. Although there are twelve reserve bank presidents, only five seats on the FOMC are reserved for them. The president of the New York Reserve Bank always occupies one of those seats, and a system of annual rotation among the other eleven reserve banks determines the occupants of the other four seats.[9] By tradition, the chairman of the BOG is also the FOMC chairman, and the FOMC vice chairman is the New York Fed president.

The decision-making board has a mixture of presidential appointees and regional representatives, both sets of whom are appointed in different ways. Why did politicians construct such a complicated appointment structure? Previous studies of the Fed's history have not directly addressed this question.

The earlier works on the Fed's origins have varying themes. Kolko (1967) subscribes to the capture theory and argues that the Fed reflected the interests of New York bankers. Livingston (1986) makes a similar argument but couched in class terms: the decline of "competitive-entrepreneurial capitalism" and the rise of the labor class forced capitalists as a class to push for the creation of the Fed as part of a larger new corporate investment system. Timberlake (1993) argues that the creation of the Fed was part of a grand development of the central banking concept in the United States. As for more political analyses, Wiebe (1962), West (1977), and White (1983) provide excellent and balanced studies of the various constellation of interests behind banking reform, but each has his own particular focus. White's study focuses on the evolution of the dual (state and national) banking system and its effects on banking reform. Wiebe studies the role of businessmen in progressive reform. His study is particularly valuable in specifying the interests of nonbanking business

---

[9] The first of the four reserve bank president seats rotates among the Federal Reserve Banks of Boston, Philadelphia, and Richmond. The second seat alternates between Cleveland and Chicago. The third seat rotates among Atlanta, Dallas, and St. Louis. The final seat rotates among Minneapolis, Kansas City, and San Francisco (Federal Reserve Act: §12A[a]).

interests. But none of these studies tackles the question of why the Fed looks as strange as it does – why the FOMC has twelve members, only seven of whom are presidential appointees; why the appointees have such long terms; why the terms are staggered; and why there is a somewhat decentralized central banking system.

An interest-based, positive explanation lurks behind the Fed's particular institutional features, including those of the structure of appointments. Broz (1999) applies such an explanation to the Fed's creation as it relates to the international currency system. He argues that the Fed was developed to create a sound payments system in the United States and to provide a basis for the establishment of the dollar as an international currency. But while Broz's perspective is the same as the one adopted in this book, the focus is different. Broz has a distinctly international focus in mind, while the focus here is more domestic – how domestic political groups helped to shape the Fed. Furthermore, while Broz seeks mostly to explain why the Fed exists at all, I focus more on why certain of the Fed's details exist in their current forms.

In answer to this third question, the study shows that the structure of Fed appointments reflects battles between Republicans and Democrats about centralization – the centralization of monetary policy-making powers in the central decision-making board versus in the branches of the central bank – and appointment power – the power of the president and Senate to appoint members of the central decision-making board.

Given the strong regional interests in the United States during the early part of the twentieth century, a traditionally centralized central bank on the model of European central banks was politically infeasible. The only attempt to create such a bank died in 1912 together with the Aldrich Bill. The subsequent plan, the Federal Reserve Act, called for a federal system of central banking, with the regional components having substantial powers to set monetary policy. Unfortunately, this system, in combination with the preferences of the appointees at the time, resulted in a Fed unwilling to actively intervene in the economy when the economy needed intervention the most – the Great Depression. The first Roosevelt administration spearheaded a movement to restructure the Fed with more power at the center. Since this restructuring in 1935, the Fed's basic structure and powers have hardly changed.

But each time the central banking system centralized or decentralized, it was accompanied by bargaining about appointment power. Prior to the Fed's creation in 1913, the Republicans repeatedly pushed for a centralized system with appointment power in the hands of New York bankers. The

Democrats pushed for a decentralized system with appointment power in the hands of the government; they got less centralization for more appointment power. In 1935, the Democrats managed to get more centralization for less appointment power. In analyzing these developments, the chapter on the Fed's history details the institutional evolution of the Fed between 1907 and 1935.

1.5 IMPLICATIONS

These three questions and their answers bring out the essential political struggles that determine monetary policy. Interbranch bargaining between the president and Senate determines the desired policy, but both must work through an appointment process that insulates the Fed from immediate influence. The Fed's insulation, however, does not mean that it is free from influence, nor does it mean that the politicians only appoint inflation hawks to the Fed – a popular misconception. As this study shows, inflation doves as well as hawks are appointed, resulting in some highly charged political conflicts within the Fed itself.

Although this book is concerned with appointment politics, there are, of course, other potential avenues of political influence on monetary policy. In addition to his formal powers, the president has some famous informal channels of influence on the Fed. Depending on the president, the Fed Chairman has weekly meetings with the president and the Treasury Secretary. At times, regular meetings of the Quadriad have occurred among the Fed, the Treasury, the Council of Economic Advisors, and the Office of Management and Budget.

Through these regular channels and more spontaneous forms of communication such as by telephone or memo, the president can potentially influence the Fed, as both anecdotal and systematic evidence seems to indicate. In one very famous example, Nixon apparently pressured Burns to inflate the economy just before the 1972 Presidential election (Borins 1972; Maisel 1973). Although some, including Burns, have denied this charge, other examples (see Greider 1987; Havrilesky 1995: 35–6) and systematic evidence in the Political Business Cycle literature support presidential and/or party influence on monetary policy (Nordhaus 1975; Hibbs 1977; Beck 1982a, 1982b; Alesina 1987; Grier 1987; Rogoff and Sibert 1988; Alesina and Roubini 1990; Alesina and Rosenthal 1995).

In addition to approving presidential nominees to the BOG, the Senate Committee on Banking, Housing, and Urban Affairs conducts semi-annual oversight hearings of the Fed's monetary policy and reviews legislation related to the Fed's structure. The semiannual oversight hearings in the Senate Banking Committee are conducted according to the Full Employment and Balanced Growth Act of 1978.[10] Under this act, the BOG submits a monetary policy report to the Senate Banking Committee every six months. In addition, the Chairman presents the report before the full Senate Committee; this presentation is often called the Humphrey-Hawkins testimony. Similar hearings also occur in the House Committee on Banking and Financial Services under the same act. These hearings usually take place in February and July of each year and are closely watched by members of the financial community.

But appointments are particularly important because they are both a regular and a formal avenue of political influence. The president may lunch with the Fed Chairman, but there is no guarantee that the Fed Chairman adheres to what the president wants. In fact, at no time does the Chairman want to give the impression to either the president or anyone else that the Fed is trying to adhere to the president's wishes; this would soil the sacred image of the Fed's independence. As for the congressional banking committees, legislation is generally not easy to pass, and even more difficult when it concerns an attack on the Fed's independence. Representative Wright Patman, a famous foe of the Fed, attempted throughout his long career to make the Fed more politically dependent in various ways, but he failed each time. As for the Humphrey-Hawkins testimonies, they are in line with Greenspan's desire to make monetary policy more transparent to the financial community and the public, rather than being a check by Congress on the Fed's policy.

In contrast, appointments are potentially powerful because the president and Senate can put in place for a long time a person who shares their views. One might argue that just as weekly lunches with the president may be ineffective, appointees can be as well. There is no commitment device to keep them from straying from the wishes of the president and Senate. But no commitment device is needed if the president and Senate are careful enough to choose someone who is not swayed from their convictions, as this book intends to show. Furthermore, there is guaranteed potential for influence every two years – the frequency of the regular appointments.

This book is inevitably informed by a rich and varied literature from a number of different fields. As a study of central banks and monetary policy, this book relates closely to the macroeconomic literature

[10] Although the act's provisions expired in 2000, both the Senate and House continue to holds these hearings under the same format as previously.

on the relationship between rational expectations and monetary policy and on central bank independence. As a study of policy delegation and bureaucracy, the book fits in with the political science studies of the political control of agencies, separation of powers, and more specifically, appointments. As a study of an institution as an object of political choice, the book connects to the growing literature in organization theory of the political foundations of institutional emergence. The book stands at the intersection of many different fields as a study of the politics of monetary policy.

The different strands of the related literature are quite complementary and have much to offer one another once the relevant connections have been made between them. First, the studies of central bank independence are largely theoretical rather than empirical, while the flip side characterizes studies of the Fed. Second, neither are much concerned with process – the principal concern of the appointments literature. Third, the normative focus of the central bank independence literature is balanced by the positive studies of the Fed and appointments. Fourth, the appointments literature has yet to examine central bank appointments that are central to works in central bank independence and the Fed. Finally, an understanding of the Fed's institutional origins would benefit from a positive analysis of institutions.

As the following chapters demonstrate, this study builds heavily on this previous body of work by attempting to make these complementary connections. First, the study is both theoretical and empirical and attempts to provide a tight connection between the two. Second, the appointment process and its relation to policy are the real foci of this study. The study looks into and illuminates the previously black box of the appointment process. Third, the study is explicitly positive – interested in what is rather than what should be. Fourth, the study examines the appointment processes of two different central banks and shows how the differences in the processes lead to different policy outcomes. Finally, I perform a positive, interest-based analysis of the Fed's origins to uncover why the appointment structure looks as it does.

These political struggles are neither unique to monetary policy nor the United States. This study attempts to shed light on the fundamental dynamics of the bargaining process and provides an approach to the study of these dynamics that can be applied in a number of different settings including the European Monetary Union (EMU).

Similar to the presidential nomination/Senate confirmation sequence in the United States, members of the ECB are nominated by the Council of Ministers and confirmed by the Heads of States. But unlike the U.S. president, the Council of Ministers' nominations are not binding; the Heads of States can suggest other nominees. Furthermore, the Heads of States must unanimously approve a nominee whereas Senate confirmation requires only a majority vote.

As the study will show, these differences have important implications for how influence occurs on policy through appointments. First, the unanimity rule makes it possible, but unlikely, for extremely inflationary countries to influence policy through appointments; when such countries prefer the current policy, the only way to satisfy them is to find another policy that satisfies them. It is more difficult for extreme politicians to exercise undue influence in the United States, because the president is only required to satisfy the Senate median rather than all the senators. Second, unanimity favors the status quo as it only takes one veto to stop policy from changing; again, because not every senator has to be satisfied in the American system, policy is easier to change. Third, even the existence of an agenda setter with binding powers is not enough on the ECB to substantially change policy. The model shows that the unanimity rule has to be changed as well.

Since the discussion for EMU began, a great deal of discussion has surrounded the entrance of traditionally inflationary countries such as Italy, Spain, Portugal, and, most recently, Greece. Although there has been much concern regarding the negative effects of these countries on monetary policy, the analysis in Chapter 5 shows that the power of one country with extreme inflation preferences is limited to conditions when all countries agree on the direction of policy change. But this is rare, and most of the time, the status quo prevails, and as Chapter 5 shows, that was the case in 1999 when EMU began. At the time, the status quo was of relatively tight policy, and thus the institutions created by the EMU founders guaranteed that Italy, Spain, and Portugal, assuming that they wanted to, could not disproportionately influence policy in order to produce easier policy.

1.6 THE PLAN OF THE BOOK

The book uses a variety of methods to tackle the three main questions. I study the Fed appointment process both theoretically and empirically with a combination of tools.

Chapter 2 develops a bargaining model of the process by which the president and the Senate appoint members to the Fed. The model lays out the policy preferences of both the president and the Senate and how those preferences become actual policy within the constraints defined by the appointment process. For each appointment opportunity, the model predicts the location of monetary policy following the appointment.

Chapter 3 provides the estimates of monetary policy preferences that are required to test the predictions from Chapter 2. For presidents, senators, and Fed members, an econometric model of voting on monetary policy is estimated using new data from the Fed's voting records and coded signals of presidential and senatorial statements regarding monetary policy. The model controls for the current economic conditions that may inspire even inflation hawks to vote for easy policy during recessions.

Chapter 4 uses the preference estimates from Chapter 3 to test the predictions from Chapter 2. From the Chapter 2 model, I derive the testable hypotheses appropriate for answering the first two questions of this book. In answer to the book's first question of whether political influence on monetary policy occurs through appointments, the results are positive; Fed appointments are a viable source of political influence on U.S. monetary policy. In answer to the second question of who influences, the results support the president always anticipating the Senate in terms of the FOMC. Dominance has less support.

Chapter 5 adapts the Chapter 2 model to the study of appointments in the new ECB. In this process, the Heads of States of the member EMU countries must unanimously approve the nominees. As a result, the model demonstrates that sometimes extremely dovish or hawkish countries could determine European monetary policy, while at other times, it is very difficult to change the current policy. Although the model lends support to recent alarm regarding the entry of high inflation countries such as Italy, preliminary results indicate that the current situation dictates against a change in the current, relatively tight policy.

Chapter 6 answers this book's third question by examining the Fed appointment process as an endogenous object of political choice. Extensive archival research is used to discover the political foundations of the Fed for its creation in 1913 and for its restructuring in 1935. The research indicates that the Fed's unusual appointment structure resulted from the battles between the Democrats and Republicans regarding the extent to which the Fed's powers were centralized. The Democrats and their constituencies of smaller banks feared a central bank controlled by big New York banks. These New York banks supported the Republicans who pushed for a real central bank. The Federal Reserve System, as established, was a compromise consisting of many smaller central banks with a central board of regional representatives as well as presidential appointees.

Chapter 7 summarizes and concludes by providing suggestions of possible extensions to other agencies and central banks. With suitable modifications, the model is applicable to any number of governmental and policy settings. The comparative possibilities are outlined in this concluding chapter.

2

A Formal Model of the Appointment Process

This chapter presents a formal model of the process by which the president and Senate appoint members to the Fed. The model lays out the president and Senate's strategic considerations when they are faced with an appointment opportunity posed by either the retirement or by the expiring term of a Fed member. The president moves first with his power of nomination and thinks about how to exploit that first-mover advantage, while the Senate tries to maximize its veto power over the president's choice of nominee. Once they agree on a nominee, the president and Senate face constraints on how far they can move Fed policy with a single appointment; the Fed's multimember decision-making structure forces the president and Senate to work around the existing Fed members. In sum, the model details how preferences work within the constraints of the appointment process to produce monetary policy.

The model encompasses several of the theories of appointments discussed in Chapter 1. The first is presidential anticipation: in the model presented here, the president always anticipates the Senate's preferences. Under a certain set of circumstances, this means that the president dominates, and at other times, the president compromises with the Senate. Under still other circumstances, neither dominates, and both in a situation of deadlock simply maintain the current policy. Thus given presidential anticipation, the model demonstrates that presidential dominance, presidential compromise, or deadlock can occur.

2.1 AN INFORMAL DESCRIPTION OF THE APPOINTMENT PROCESS

This book focuses on the BOG appointments as they affect policy made by the FOMC; the study takes as given the appointees for the reserve banks presidents. The appointment process used to appoint BOG members follows the general presidential nomination-Senate confirmation sequence prescribed in Article II, Section 2 of the U.S. Constitution. The only special feature of the process is a prescription of the Federal Reserve Act: the president must give consideration to representation of the twelve reserve districts and "fair representation of the financial, agricultural, industrial, and commercial interests and geographical divisions of the country" (Federal Reserve Act §10 ¶1, 38 Stat. 251(1913), 12 U.S.C. §241(1935)). Informally, consideration is given to the preferences of individual senators, financial sector opinions, and the candidate's sex and race (Havrilesky 1995: 291, 296–7; Jones 1995: 69).

The president submits his nominee to the Senate which refers the nomination to its Committee on Banking and Urban Affairs.[11] The Banking Committee investigates and holds hearings to question the nominee. Committee members often ask candidates about potential conflicts of financial interest and about their policy views. The Committee usually considers BOG candidates with nominees for other official posts related to the financial industry (e.g., commissioners for the Securities and Exchange Commission). The Banking Committee then votes to recommend the nominee to the full Senate. If the nominee makes it through committee, the full Senate debates and votes to confirm the nominee. To date, neither the Banking Committee nor the full Senate has formally rejected a nominee to the BOG. In fact, the Senate has confirmed most nominees by unanimous consent (Morris 1991: 31).

To summarize, the president chooses a candidate, the Senate Banking Committee votes to recommend the nominee, and the full Senate then decides whether to confirm the appointment. The following model attempts to capture the key features of this process.

2.2 THE APPOINTMENT PROCESS MODEL

2.2.1 *Assumptions and Definitions*

1. Actors and their preferences. There are three sets of actors in the following model: presidents, Senate Banking Committee members, and FOMC members (Table 2.1).

---

[11] The Banking Committee usually consists of eighteen members, a majority of whom are from the majority party.

Table 2.1: *Acronyms, Variables, and Other Notations*

FOMC	Federal Open Market Committee
BOG	Board of Governors
P	President's ideal point
S	Senate Banking Committee median's ideal point
SQ0	FOMC median before a retirement
SQ1	FOMC median after a retirement
SQ2	FOMC median after the new appointee takes office
x1,..., x12	FOMC members numbered in order of easiest to tightest policy
y	FOMC retiree
x	New appointee
SQ⁻	Senate's indifference point
L	Lower limit of the range of possible outcomes
H	Upper limit of the range of possible outcomes

I assume that all actors have well-behaved, single-peaked preferences over a single dimension of monetary policy measured by the federal funds rate, $r \in [0, 1]$; lower rates indicate easier policy. The utility for an individual i is a monotone, decreasing function, θ, of the distance of her ideal point, r_i, from the current Fed policy, $SQ : U_i(r_i, SQ) = \theta(|r_i - SQ|)$.

As the statistical model of preferences makes clearer in Chapter 3, r_i measures at any time an individual's leaning toward easier or tighter policy as a function of the individual's characteristics and economic conditions. Volcker and Seger's r_is tell us that Seger is *always* easier than Volcker. Because r_i is a function of economic conditions, one can also think of r_i as an implied catch-all for common economic outcomes such as inflation. Thus Volcker is always an inflation hawk relative to Seger.

2. *Actions.* First, the president chooses a nominee, x, on the set of $r \in [0, 1]$; the nominee maps to a specific FOMC median, $SQ2$. Section 2.2.4 describes the exact mapping. Second, the Senate accepts or rejects the nominee. Third, the FOMC members vote on monetary policy according to the rule: Vote = tighter policy if $r_i > SQ$, Vote = easier policy, otherwise.

3. *Other assumptions and implications*

THE SENATE BANKING COMMITTEE AND THE FOMC. Because both the Senate Banking Committee and the FOMC are majority rule institutions, it follows from the preceding assumptions, plus the assumption of perfect and complete information, that the median voter theorem applies to both these collective institutions; the Senate Banking Committee median (S) and the FOMC median (SQ) capture the policy positions of the two institutions.

I assume further that the Banking Committee median accurately represents the Senate floor median; hereafter all references to the Senate are to the Senate Banking Committee. Although there is some theoretical and empirical controversy regarding this assumption, Krehbiel (1990) and Krehbiel and Rivers' (1988) results support the assumption. In particular, Krehbiel (1990) shows, using a variety of interest group ratings, that many committees, including the Senate Banking Committee, are not preference outliers compared to the floor. Krehbiel and Rivers (1988) focus on the Senate Committee on Labor and Human Resources since they are concerned with minimum wage law.

The FOMC median, the current Fed policy or SQ, is the median of the members *currently serving* on the FOMC. When a vacancy occurs, in the absence of an appointment, the FOMC continues to function with the reduced membership.[12] With an odd number of members, the median member is the FOMC median. With an even number of members, I designate the midpoint between the two middle members as the median.

Despite the conventional wisdom of the all-powerful Fed chair, the FOMC median is a reasonable proxy for the institution for several reasons. First, the chair has agenda-setting powers, but those powers are limited. In a typical FOMC meeting, the chair begins with his assessment of the current economy and provides options regarding the amount by which the FOMC might want to change interest rates. Each member then reacts and adds to the chair's comments, and in light of their comments, the chair may adjust his proposal. Once the chair is satisfied that his proposal has at least majority support, he calls for a vote.[13] Thus the chair's agenda-setting power is neither exclusive nor absolute; others can help set the agenda, and the chair engages in an intrameeting adjustment process for his own agenda.

Second, even if the chair has agenda-setting power, he must satisfy the median. Suppose the reversion point is the median – the policy starting

---

[12] Seven FOMC members constitute a quorum.
[13] I thank the research staff at the Minneapolis Fed for information on the FOMC meetings.

point.[14] For an odd number of FOMC members, the chair cannot move the outcome away from the median member because he cannot obtain majority support for any other proposal.

The same is true for an even-numbered FOMC, for example with twelve members. In that case, the reversion point is also the median, but the median is now the *range* between the sixth and seventh members; any given realization of the median is a random draw from that range. If the chair is to the left of the sixth member, he cannot obtain any point to the left of the range's midpoint, because the seventh member would reject that point. The seventh member would be better off with the status quo because it guarantees that at least some draws of the median are right of the midpoint, closer to her ideal point. Thus the best the chair can do is to choose the midpoint itself, which guarantees that the outcome is always at the midpoint rather than to the right of the midpoint some of the time.[15] The seventh member accepts the midpoint because she is indifferent between the midpoint and the status quo; in expectation, they yield the same utility.[16]

Third, the empirical evidence for chair agenda-setting power is mixed at best. If the chair has much agenda-setting power, his voting weight should be higher compared to that of the other members. Krause (1994) finds support for the chair's ability to build consensus, and Chappell, McGregor, and Vermilyea (1998) conclude that the chair's voting weight is higher than that of typical FOMC members. However, Chappell, McGregor, and Vermilyea (1998) also conclude that the median voter theorem, which presupposes equal voting weights, accurately represents FOMC voting behavior. Furthermore, Chappell, Havrilesky, and McGregor (1993: 203; 1995: 123) find that they cannot reject the hypothesis of equal chair voting weight.[17]

---

[14] Given the median voter theorem, the assumption is reasonable.

[15] Although the policy outcome point – the FOMC median – does not change, the actual Fed policy can still change. Depending on the economic situation, the same median point can mean raising interest rates fifty basis points or lowering them twenty-five basis points. The context will translate the median point to the real policy at a particular point in time.

[16] Essentially, the foregoing is an application of the RR (1978) setter game in which one player is a majority rule body and the starting point is the median. In this setup, the median always prevails, although this is not the case if the median is not the starting point.

[17] The extent to which these studies arrive at different conclusions is disconcerting. The mixed results may have to do with the use of different sources of data and testing methods. The debate might be settled when the Fed finally releases all of the minutes

The remaining evidence regarding chair power is anecdotal, but even anecdotes provide mixed evidence. According to Greider (1987: 639–40), Volcker was informally outvoted in 1987: "The sharp division in the Federal Open Market Committee was not revealed by the final vote or by the FOMC's minutes. The chairman himself did not normally dissent, even when he did not get his way ... *Volcker yielded to the others*," (p. 640, emphasis added). Rose (1974: 187–8) claims that Burns was formally outvoted on a number of occasions. These anecdotes indicate that the chair does not always have his way with the other FOMC members, but rather, it may be the other way around.

APPOINTMENTS AND POLICY. As the utility function reflects, actors care only about policy – not about specific appointments; they care about appointments only insofar as they affect policy. But policy, the end goal, is produced by the FOMC, while appointments, the means to the ends, are on the BOG. How can the president and Senate ensure policy effects on the FOMC through BOG appointments?

Essentially the president and Senate can manipulate FOMC policy with their BOG appointments because the BOG members make up a majority of the FOMC. I assume that the president and Senate are perfectly informed about the preferences of current and future reserve bank presidents. Because reserve bank presidents often serve multiple five-year terms, and this system of rotation is fixed, the assumption is reasonable. For example, the Philadelphia reserve bank president recently retired after nineteen years of service – nearly four consecutive terms.

2.2.2 *The Sequence*

The *appointment process model* is a spatial bargaining game between the president and the Senate. The game begins when a member of the FOMC leaves. The president moves first with his choice of appointee, after which the Senate can veto the choice. Once they agree on an appointee, the appointment is made, a new policy outcome is realized (the resulting FOMC median), and payoffs are distributed to the president and Senate based on the new outcome. If they fail to agree on an appointee, the

from its meetings. With the voting records from the publicly available "Record of Policy Actions," the data used in this study, a true test of the chair's agenda-setting power is not possible. The record does not provide enough information on the deliberations prior to the vote, and the votes already reflect chair influence. The minutes of the meetings do not suffer from this limitation. Chappell, McGregor, and Vermilyea (1998) use the currently available set of minutes to conduct their test.

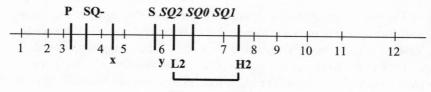

Figure 2.1: Example

president and Senate have to put up with the median of the eleven-member FOMC – the reversion point.

2.2.3 An Example

Before describing the equilibria of the game more generally, consider the example in Figure 2.1. We need the following definitions.

Retirees and nominees. Define y as the retiree, and x as the nominee or if approved – the appointee.

Status quos. $SQ0$ is the median of the FOMC *before* any given retirement, $SQ1$ is the FOMC median *after* the retirement, and $SQ2$ is the FOMC median after an appointee takes her seat on the FOMC.

Policy outcome. $SQ2$ is the policy outcome.

Reversion point. $SQ1$ is the reversion point.

The Senate's indifference point. The Senate's indifference point, SQ^-, is the point at which it is indifferent between SQ^- and $SQ1 : |S - SQ1| = |S - SQ^-|$.

FOMC members. The FOMC members are labeled $\{x1, \ldots, x12\}$ in order of easier to tighter monetary policy. In Figure 2.1, the x's for the FOMC members have been dropped for ease of explication.

Range of possible outcomes. The range of possible outcomes is the range in which the president and Senate can move the FOMC median with a given single appointment. L is the lower limit, and H is the upper limit of the range.

In this example, the president (P) and the Senate Banking Committee median (S) favor easier policy relative to the current status quo, $SQ0$.

The appointment process begins with a retirement, $y = x6$. After the retirement, the FOMC median immediately changes from $SQ0$ to $SQ1 = x7$, which is the reversion point, the outcome that the president and Senate must tolerate in the absence of an agreement.

If we compare P, S, and $SQ1$ and forget momentarily about the other FOMC members, the president and Senate would agree on the Senate's indifference point, SQ^-, as the policy outcome. The president would suggest this point as the agenda setter, and the Senate would agree to it because it is indifferent between SQ^- and $SQ1$. So far, the game is a straightforward application of the Romer and Rosenthal (1978) setter game.

However, SQ^- lies outside the possible range of outcomes for the retirement, $y = x6$. For this retirement, whether the nominee's ideal point is $x5$ or $x1$, the lowest point the president and Senate can achieve with this single appointment is $L2 > SQ^-$. In this manner, $L2$ defines the lower boundary of the range of *possible* outcomes. The upper boundary, $H2 = \frac{x7+x8}{2}$, results from an appointment to the right of $x8$. $[L2, H2]$ is the entire range of possible outcomes for $y = x6$.

The president and Senate still want to get as close as possible to SQ^-. In the range of possible outcomes, that point is $L2$ – the *actual* outcome. Formally, the equilibrium of this particular game is defined on the path by the president's nominee choice, $x \leq x5$ and the Senate's acceptance. The president and Senate receive payoffs based on $SQ2 = \frac{x5+x7}{2}$.

2.2.4 *Possible Outcomes*

I now generalize the example by first examining all the possible outcomes and then adding the president and Senate to the analysis and seeing what it means for the actual outcomes.

The example illustrates that the game is relatively simple except for the mapping of appointees to policy outcomes – the FOMC medians. First, a single appointee's position, x, is never the policy outcome of the game. In the preceding example, even if $x6$ is the retiree, and x is between $x5$ and $x7$, the new policy outcome would be $\frac{x+x7}{2}$ rather than x.

Second, even though x itself can never be the policy outcome, x may define a unique policy outcome, that is the correspondence between x and $SQ2$ can be unique. However, at other times, the correspondence between x and $SQ2$ is not one to one; a range of appointees leads to the same outcome. Going back to the example, when $x6$ leaves, any new x such that $x5 < x < x7$ will determine a unique policy outcome defined by $\frac{x+x7}{2}$. The same is true for any x such that $x7 < x < x8$; the outcome in this case will be $\frac{x+x7}{2}$. However, any appointee greater than $x8$ will not result in a unique policy outcome. In fact, all such appointees will result in the *same* outcome, $\frac{x7+x8}{2}$. Similarly, all appointees less than $x5$ will result in the same outcome, $\frac{x5+x7}{2}$.

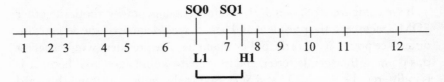

Figure 2.2: Range 1

These complications will affect the extent to which the president and Senate can move policy to exactly their desired location with one appointment. Sometimes, no matter how much they would like to move policy to some location, there will be a limit to which they can do so, and the limit will be determined by the location of the vacancy.

In this subsection, I formally characterize the limits – the range of possible outcomes for any given vacancy. The possible outcomes are grouped into four ranges based on seat numbers: the first five seats, seat 6, seat 7, and the last five. Range 1 is defined as $[L1, H1]$, Range 2 as $[L2, H2]$, and so on.

Range 1 (Figure 2.2): *if* $y \in \{x1, x2, x3, x4, x5\}$

Range 1 is defined by a vacancy in one of the first five FOMC seats. Once one of $\{x1, x2, x3, x4, x5\}$ retires, the FOMC median will immediately move to $SQ1 = x7$.

The first two sets of possible appointees do not uniquely define the outcome, $SQ2$. First, in (1) in the following text, all appointments to the left of $x6$ ($x \leq x6$) will result in $SQ0$, the same median before the retirement of the outgoing member. Thus $SQ0$ defines the lower limit, $L1$, to which the president and Senate may move policy with any one such retirement. Second, in (2), any appointment to the right of $x8$ will result in the median defined by the mean between the 7th and 8th FOMC members. This point defines the upper limit, $H1$, to which the president and Senate may move policy with any one such retirement. To formalize, the nonunique correspondences between x and $SQ2$ are defined by:

$$(1)\ x \leq x6 \quad \Rightarrow \quad SQ2 = SQ0 = L1$$

$$(2)\ x \geq x8 \quad \Rightarrow \quad SQ2 = \frac{x7 + x8}{2} = H1$$

The second set of possible appointees, between seats 6 and 8, do define a unique set of outcomes – the mean of the new appointee and the 7th member. The new outcome will be between the lower and upper

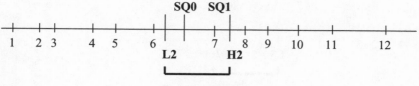

Figure 2.3: Range 2

limits. The unique one-to-one correspondences between x and $SQ2$ are defined by:

$$(3)\ x6 < x < x8 \quad \Rightarrow L1 < \quad SQ2 = \frac{x + x7}{2} < H1$$

Thus the complete range of outcomes for $y \in \{x1, \ldots, x5\}$ is $L1 \le SQ2 \le H2$. Whether a one-to-one correspondence exists depends on whether x is between or outside the boundaries defined by seats 6 and 8.

Range 2 (Figure 2.3): *if $y \in \{x6\}$*

Because $x6$ and $x7$ define the FOMC median, a retirement of $x6$ or $x7$ means that the president and Senate can potentially change the outcome to a greater extent compared to when the other members retire. For example, if $x5$ rather than $x6$ retires, the president and Senate will always bump up against the lower limit, L, defined in part by $x6$: $L = SQ0 = \frac{x6+x}{2}$. When $x6$ retires, $x5$ defines the lower limit rather than $x6$, and thus the lower limit is lower, and the range is larger.

If $x6$ retires, $SQ1 = x7$. As in Range 1, there are two sets of possible outcomes based on the placement of the new appointee.
The first set defines the nonunique correspondences between an appointee and outcomes:

$$(1)\ x \le x5 \quad \Rightarrow \quad SQ2 = \frac{x5 + x7}{2} = L2 \le L1$$

$$(2)\ x \ge x8 \quad \Rightarrow \quad SQ2 = \frac{x7 + x8}{2} = H2 = H1$$

In (1), since $x5 \le x6$, this lower limit will be lower than in Range 1: $L2 < L1$. According to (2), the upper limit stays the same: $H1 = H2$. In sum, Range 1 $\le$ Range 2.

The second set defines the unique outcomes. When x is between $x5$ and $x8$, x together with $x7$ will define the new outcome:

$$(3)\ x5 < x < x8 \quad \Rightarrow \quad L2 < SQ2 = \frac{x + x7}{2} < H2$$

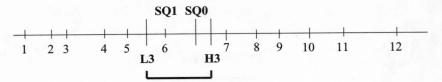

Figure 2.4: Range 3

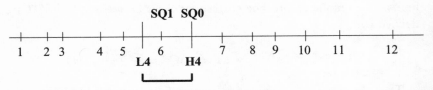

Figure 2.5: Range 4

Thus the complete range of outcomes for $y \in \{x6\}$ is $L2 \leq SQ2 \leq H2$, where $L2 \leq L1$ and $H1 = H2$ such that Range 1 $\leq$ Range 2.

Range 3 (Figure 2.4): *if* $y \in \{x7\}$

Analogous reasoning applies to Ranges 3 and 4 in which $y \in \{x7, \ldots, x12\}$. In order to be complete, I quickly provide the formal details.

For any $y \in \{x7\}$, $SQ1 = x6$. The nonunique correspondences between x and $SQ2$ are defined for any x such that:

$$(1) \; x \leq x5 \quad \Rightarrow \quad SQ2 = \frac{x5 + x6}{2} = L3$$

$$(2) \; x \geq x8 \quad \Rightarrow \quad SQ2 = \frac{x6 + x8}{2} = H3$$

The unique correspondences are:

$$(3) \; x5 \leq x \leq x8 \quad \Rightarrow \quad L3 < SQ2 = \frac{x + x6}{2} < H3$$

Thus the total range of outcomes for $y \in \{x7\}$ is $L4 \leq SQ2 \leq H4$.

Range 4 (Figure 2.5): *if* $y \in \{x8, x9, x10, x11, x12\}$

For any $y \in \{x8, \ldots, x12\}$, $SQ1 = x6$. The nonunique correspondences between x and $SQ2$ are defined for any x such that:

$$(1) \; x \leq x5 \quad \Rightarrow \quad SQ2 = \frac{x5 + x6}{2} = L4 = L3$$

$$(2) \; x \geq x7 \quad \Rightarrow \quad SQ2 = SQ0 = H4 \leq H3$$

The unique correspondences are defined for any x such that:

$$(3)\ x5 < x < x7 \quad \Rightarrow \quad L3 < SQ2 = \frac{x + x6}{2} < H3$$

Thus the total range of outcomes for $y \in \{x8, \ldots, x12\}$ is $L3 \leq SQ2 \leq H3$ where $L3$ is the same as $L4$ but $H3 \geq H4$, and Range 3 $\geq$ Range 4. As with the retirement of $x6$, $x7$'s retirement, compared to the other members' retirements, leaves the president and Senate more latitude to move policy.

2.2.5 *Actual Outcomes: Adding the President and the Senate*

In the previous section, I examined the entire range of *possible* outcomes for a single appointment given the location of the vacancy. In this section, I predict the location of the *actual* outcomes in the range of possible outcomes by adding the president and Senate to the analysis. The actual outcomes are determined by the three possible orderings of the president and Senate relative to $SQ1$.

Case 1: Presidential Dominance

DEFINITION. *Romer-Rosenthal (RR) equilibrium policy.* The RR equilibrium policy is the game's outcome in the absence of the constraints imposed by the range of possible outcomes, for example SQ^- in the example. The RR equilibrium policy is the Romer-Rosenthal setter game (1978) equilibrium.

In Case 1, the president is closer to the status quo, $SQ1$, than the Senate. As the agenda setter, the president can propose his ideal point, P, as the *RR equilibrium policy*, and the Senate will accept the proposal as the outcome will be closer to its ideal point, S, than the status quo, $SQ1$. The problem is that P might be outside the range of possible outcomes. In that case, whichever boundary point, L or H, is closer to the president's ideal point will become the actual policy outcome.

More formally, there are two possible configurations of this case. In each configuration, $|P - SQ1| < |S - SQ1|$.

(1) $S < P < SQ1 \quad \Rightarrow \quad SQ2 = P$ if $P \in [L, H]$, $SQ2 = L$ *otherwise*

(2) $SQ1 < P < S \quad \Rightarrow \quad SQ2 = P$ if $P \in [L, H]$, $SQ2 = H$ *otherwise*

Case 2: Presidential Compromise. In this case, the Senate is closer than the president to the status quo, $SQ1$. However, the ultimate policy outcome depends on how close the Senate is to the president. In some cases

(Case 2a), the Senate is closer to the president than the Senate's indifference point, SQ^-, and in those cases, the president has every incentive to propose his ideal point as the RR equilibrium policy which the Senate has no reason to reject because the reversion point, the status quo point, $SQ1$, is farther away from S than P. In other cases (Case 2b), the Senate's indifference point is closer than the Senate's ideal point to the president, and the president will propose SQ^- as the RR equilibrium policy; the Senate will accept as it is indifferent, by definition, between SQ^- and the status quo.

As before, the actual outcome will be whichever is possible: a boundary point or P in the first set of cases (Case 2a), and a boundary point or SQ^- in the second set of cases (Case 2b).

There are four possible configurations of Case 2. In each configuration, $|S - SQ1| < |P - SQ1|$.

Case 2a: S is closer to P than to SQ1

(1) $P < S < SQ1$ and $S < \dfrac{P + SQ1}{2}$

$\Rightarrow \quad SQ2 = P$ if $P \in [L, H], SQ2 = L$ *otherwise*

(2) $SQ1 < S < P$ and $S > \dfrac{P + SQ1}{2}$

$\Rightarrow \quad SQ2 = P$ if $P \in [L, H], SQ2 = H$ *otherwise*

Case 2b: S is closer to SQ1 than to P

(3) $P < S < SQ1$ and $S > \dfrac{P + SQ1}{2}$

$\Rightarrow \quad SQ2 = SQ^-$ if $SQ^- \in [L, H], \quad SQ2 = L$ *otherwise*

(4) $SQ1 < S < P$ and $S < \dfrac{P + SQ1}{2}$

$\Rightarrow \quad SQ2 = SQ^-$ if $SQ^- \in [L, H], \quad SQ2 = H$ *otherwise*

Note that although S is closer to $SQ1$ than to P in Case 2, the president still dominates in configurations (1) and (2). This is due to the president's agenda-setting power which also shows its advantages in the Senate's inability to get its ideal point, S; at best, the Senate can obtain SQ^-.

Case 3: Deadlock. In this case, the status quo lies between the president and Senate's ideal points. Thus, neither the president or Senate is willing to give up ground, because one's gain is the other's loss. They therefore agree to disagree; they maintain the current FOMC median. $SQ1$ is the RR equilibrium policy.

There are two possible configurations in this case:

$$(1)\ P < SQ1 < S \quad \Rightarrow \quad SQ2 = SQ1$$
$$(2)\ S < SQ1 < P \quad \Rightarrow \quad SQ2 = SQ1$$

The President's Influence. All in all, the president maintains much influence over the process even in this model of presidential anticipation. Essentially he gains leverage from his first-mover advantage. In Case 1, if the Senate moved first rather than the president, the outcomes would be either S or the president's indifference point, much as the current Case 2 is favorable toward the president. In Case 2, the outcome would be S rather than P or SQ^-; there would be Senate dominance. But in the current constitutional setup, because the president is the agenda setter, he can use this advantage in order to obtain a point closer to or identical to his ideal point in either of the first two cases. In Case 3, who moves first does not matter because $SQ1$ is always the outcome.

2.3 AN EXTENSION OF THE MODEL TO MULTIPLE APPOINTMENTS

In this section, I briefly consider an extension to the model. I consider how the model would change if the president and Senate were to look ahead and bargain over a series of appointments rather than a single appointment. In the Appendix, I consider a second extension of the model to the BOG.

In the previous setup, the president and Senate played a new appointment process game each time a new vacancy occurred on the FOMC. It is interesting to consider what would happen if all of these games were linked sequentially for a given president and Senate.

Assume for simplicity that there is no discounting and that the president and the Senate can foresee the upcoming retirements; as the term lengths are for fixed periods, the assumption is reasonable.[18] Also assume that the utilities of the presidents and senators are now based on an average of payoffs from all the games they play; this assumption takes into account the game's total additive payoffs given that the original utility function is a loss function with negative payoffs. Formally, $U = \frac{1}{T} \sum_T \theta(|r_i - SQ_t|)$, where t denotes an iteration of the game. If this particular president and Senate has three appointment opportunities, for example, we would like

---

[18] Furthermore, early retirements are also usually known in advance.

to know how the third appointment conditions the choice of the second, and how the second conditions the first.

In this modified setup, there are two possible changes to the original model. First, the exact placement of the appointees may matter more than previously. Referring to the example in Figure 2.1, the president and Senate would previously appoint anyone to the left of $x5$ ($x \leq x5$) in order to achieve $SQ2 = L2$, which is as close as possible to SQ^-, the RR equilibrium policy. With multiple appointments, placements of appointees between SQ^- and $x5$ could impede future progress toward SQ^-. Therefore, the president and Senate appoint members right at SQ^- if no member is at that point, or if there is already a member at SQ^-, they will appoint members at or to the left of SQ^- in order to maximize the future chances of getting exactly to SQ^-. Thus in general, the president and Senate will try to appoint members on or as near as possible to the RR equilibrium policy point: P in Case 1, P or SQ^- in Case 2, and $SQ1$ in Case 3.

Second, the president and Senate may never reach the long-run equilibrium point even with multiple appointment opportunities. Going back to the example, if a second appointment opportunity opened up at $x10$, $SQ1$ will become $x5$. This then creates a deadlock situation with P and S on either side of $SQ1 = x5$. The president and Senate will not be able to agree on policy changes and will maintain the outcome at $x5$ with this and any future appointments. Thus progress toward SQ^- will stop at $x5$.

In the two consecutive appointment opportunities described, note that the appointee was $x \leq x5$ for the first appointment opportunity, and $x5$ for the second. Interestingly, we have come full circle: the original static model also predicts $x \leq x5$ for the first appointment, and if the same president and Senate play a second appointment game after the first, then $x = SQ1 = x5$, as they will be in a deadlock situation. Thus without reference to the second game conditioning the first game, the predictions are the same from the original static model versus those of the more dynamic version considered in this section.

2.4 SUMMARY

This chapter has developed a model of the process to appoint members to the Fed: both the FOMC and the BOG (in the Appendix). The model is similar to the Romer and Rosenthal (1978) setter game except that the multimember structure of the FOMC imposes limits on the extent to which the politicians can make progress toward the RR equilibrium policy.

The model makes clear, testable predictions about the location of policy after a new appointee takes office based on the preferences of the president, Senate, and the existing Fed members. In order to test these predictions, we need a measure of preferences over monetary policy and a method to estimate the ideal points – the aim of the next chapter.

2.5 APPENDIX: THE BOARD OF GOVERNORS

The appointment process model easily extends to the seven-member BOG with three slight modifications due to the odd rather than even number of members on the BOG. First, $SQ0$ and $SQ2$ are defined by a single member, $x4$, on the seven-member BOG, and $SQ1$ is defined by the two middle members of the after-retirement, six-member BOG.

Second, there are only three rather than four ranges of possible outcomes. The original four ranges for the FOMC are based on four groupings of the twelve FOMC seats: the group of seats to the left of the median ($x \leq x5$), each of the two seats that make up the FOMC median ($x6$ and $x7$), and the final group of seats to the right of the median ($x \geq x8$). Because the BOG contains an odd number of members, the median is defined by a single member, $x4$, rather than two members as previously. Therefore, the middle range is reduced from two ranges to one defined by the vacancy of $x4$. The ranges based on the left and right sides of the median are virtually the same except for a smaller number of seats. Range 1 is $y \in \{x1, x2, x3\}$, Range 2 is $y \in \{x4\}$, and Range 3 is $y \in \{x5, x6, x7\}$.

Third, because a single member defines the median, x can become the outcome of the game.

The definitions of the limits are analogous to those of the FOMC ranges with slight differences.

Range 1: *if* $y \in \{x1, x2, x3\}$

For any $y \in \{x1, x2, x3\}$, $SQ1 = \frac{x4+x5}{2}$. The nonunique correspondences between x and $SQ2$ are defined for any x such that:

$$(1)\, x \leq x4 \quad \Rightarrow \quad SQ2 = x4 = SQ0 = L1$$
$$(2)\, x \geq x5 \quad \Rightarrow \quad SQ2 = x5 = H1$$

The unique correspondences are defined for any x such that:

$$(3)\, x4 \leq x \leq x5 \quad \Rightarrow \quad L1 \leq SQ2 = x \leq H1$$

Range 2: *if* $y \in \{x4\}$

For any $y \in \{x\}$, $SQ1 = \frac{x3+x5}{2}$. The nonunique correspondences are:

$$(1)\, x \le x3 \quad \Rightarrow \quad SQ2 = x3 = L2 < L1$$
$$(2)\, x \ge x5 \quad \Rightarrow \quad SQ2 = x5 = H2 = H1$$

The unique correspondences are:

$$(3)\, x3 \le x \le x5 \quad \Rightarrow \quad L2 \le SQ2 = x \le H2$$

Range 3: *if* $y \in \{x5, x6, x7\}$

For any $y \in \{x5, x6, x7\}$, $SQ1 = \frac{x3+x4}{2}$. The nonunique correspondences are:

$$(1)\, x \le x3 \quad \Rightarrow \quad SQ2 = x3 = L3 = L2 < L1$$
$$(2)\, x \ge x4 \quad \Rightarrow \quad SQ2 = x4 = H3 < H1 = H2$$

The unique correspondences are:

$$(3)\, x3 \le x4 \quad \Rightarrow \quad L3 \le SQ2 = x \le H3$$

In overall comparisons, Range 2 is the largest of the three. Whether Range 1 is greater than Range 3 and vice versa depends on the distance between $x4$ and $x5$ for Range 1 and between $x3$ and $x4$ for Range 3.

Adding the president and Senate is totally analogous to the FOMC game; either the RR equilibrium policy or the boundary points will prevail.

3

Estimating Monetary Policy Preferences

Testing the implications of the appointment process model requires estimates of monetary policy ideal points for presidents, Senate Banking Committee members, and FOMC members. In this chapter I develop a method to estimate those ideal points.

3.1 THE BASIC PROBLEMS

3.1.1 Problem 1: Economic Conditions

The first problem of estimating monetary policy preferences is the confounding of ideal points with economic conditions. In monetary policy, the economic context of voting leads to highly similar voting patterns for very different individuals. Those patterns make it difficult to differentiate among individuals with commonly used measures such as vote proportions.

Take the example of Nancy Teeters and Henry Wallich. President Carter appointed Teeters to the BOG in 1978. As a member of the FOMC, Teeters was a well-known easy-policy advocate in contrast to Henry Wallich, a staunch tight-policy supporter, who was appointed in 1974 (Greider 1987: 72, 81, 465–6). Despite their differences, both Teeters and Wallich consistently voted for tighter monetary policy during 1978–82, a period of very high inflation.[19] As a result, Teeters and Wallich appear over their careers to have very similar monetary policy preferences based on a vote proportion measure:[20] Teeters' vote proportion was 0.51 from

---

[19] Annual rate of 13.1 percent for the United States in 1980 (OECD 1997: A19): the highest level since World War II.
[20] An individual's tight policy votes divided by the total number of her votes.

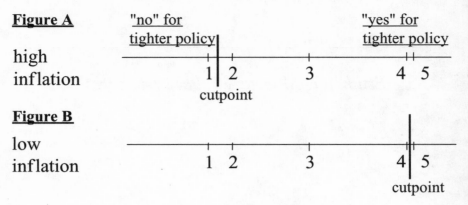

Figure 3.1: Ideal Points and Cutpoints

1978 to 1984, and Wallich's was 0.61 from 1974 to 1986. On the BOG, they are right next to each other in a rank ordering of all seven contemporary members. Basically, because of inflation, Teeters had few opportunities to vote for easy policy even if she wanted to, and the same is true in the other direction for Wallich who faced a severe recession during 1975–6 and in 1980.

The problem is that vote proportions discard useable information regarding the economic context of voting. Vote proportions average across the votes and therefore, across the economic shifts. Thus two individuals with the same voting record will have the same vote proportion regardless of when they served. However, the "when" matters a great deal. If an individual votes for tight policy all the time, our insights should be different if she served during inflationary times as opposed to recessionary times.

In sum we need to know how the conditions during the time of service skews votes in one direction or the other. The method in this chapter uses a statistical model that controls for the economic swings. As in Figure 3.1, the model works on the idea that cutpoints shift across individuals who have fixed ideal points.

3.1.2 *Problem 2: Comparisons across Time and Institutions*

The second problem of estimating monetary policy preferences is the comparison of individuals across time and across the three institutions of the presidency, Senate, and the Fed.

The appointment process model requires comparisons of Fed members appointed on different dates. For example, in order to assess the impact of Martha Seger's 1984 appointment to replace Nancy Teeters (appointed August 1978), it is necessary not only to compare both Seger and Teeters to one another, but also to the previous appointees who were serving on the BOG: Rice (April 1979), Volcker (July 1979), Martin (January 1982), Partee (December 1975), Gramley (February 1980), and Wallich (January 1974). The rank orderings of these appointees determines the Fed median – a crucial variable in the formal model. The preceding also applies to the Senate median.

The appointment process model also requires comparisons of individuals from three different institutions. In the model, the locations of the president, the Senate median, and the FOMC median relative to one another determines the predicted locations of the new appointee and the resulting FOMC median. Testing the model therefore requires estimating ideal points for all three sets of actors on one common scale.

3.2 THE PREFERENCE ESTIMATION MODEL

The method in this chapter tackles both problems of estimating monetary policy preferences. First, in dealing with the current economic conditions, the method uses a fixed effects model with two sets of variables that isolate the effects of individual characteristics from the time-specific economic conditions. I use the coefficients on the individual characteristics as ideal points estimates.

Second, with respect to producing estimates comparable across time, the coefficients on the individual characteristics are not time-specific. On comparing across institutions, the method uses one institution, the FOMC, to bridge across the three institutions. Because presidents and senators take positions on FOMC votes, the FOMC provides a common scale for all three sets of ideal points. This feature is analogous to Bailey and Chang's (2001) work on the Supreme Court in which the president takes positions on Supreme Court and Senate votes. The difference is that in their setup, the bridge actor, the president, actively takes positions in the other arenas; whereas in this setting, the other arenas' actors take positions in the bridge actor's arena. Thus the bridge actor's role in one setup is opposite to her role in the other setup.

3.2.1 Assumptions

As in Chapter 2, I assume that the true underlying monetary policy preferences of each actor, i ($i \in \{1, \ldots, N\}$), are defined on a single dimension of

Table 3.1: *Notation*

r = federal funds rate
t = time of meeting (t = 1, ..., T)
i = index for individual i (i = 1, ..., N)
α_i = set of coefficients on dummy variables equal to 1 for member i, 0 otherwise
x_t = set of macroeconomic variables
β = set of coefficients on x_t
ε_{it} = error term

easier to tighter monetary policy as measured by a lower or higher federal funds rate, r. Each individual has an ideal federal funds rate, r_i. We are interested in estimating r_i for presidents, senators, and FOMC members. (See Table 3.1 for notation.)

It seems reasonable to assume that each individual has a core set of characteristics that do not vary according to the current economic conditions. Thus when inflation is high, even if individuals all vote for tighter policy, they will still vary in the extent to which they desire tighter policy. Although Teeters and Wallich voted identically to tighten policy in the late 70s, no one would claim that these two individuals shared the same monetary policy philosophy. As the economy came out of recession in the 80s, their different core views on policy revealed themselves in opposing votes.

I therefore further assume that r_i is related to (1) a set of macroeconomic variables (e.g., inflation, Gross Domestic Product [GDP] growth, unemployment) and (2) a set of individual variables (e.g., political affiliation, education, and years in government). The macroeconomic variables are time-specific to each FOMC meeting, t ($t \in \{1, ..., T\}$) but not individual-specific. Conversely, the individual variables are individual-specific but not time-specific.

The separation of these variable types is an attempt to capture the following assumed sequence of events: (1) the individual observes the current macroeconomic conditions, (2) she processes these observations with her characteristics, then (3) she arrives at her ideal federal funds rate for time t.

As a function of economic conditions, r_i is a catch-all for common economic outcomes such as inflation, unemployment, and output. In other words, r_i is not just the preferred federal funds rate, but also the preferred inflation rate, unemployment rate, and growth rate.

3.2.2 The Model

If the current economic conditions affect individuals equally, the conditions should scale up or down all ideal points, r_is, by the same amount. As required, in the following model, any change in x_t affects each individual's ideal point, r_i, by the same amount, β:

$$r_{it} = \alpha_i + \beta' x_t + \epsilon_{it} \tag{3.1}$$

where α_i is a coefficient on a dummy variable for individual i, x_t is a $K \times 1$ vector of macroeconomic variables, β is the $K \times 1$ corresponding vector of coefficients, and ϵ_{it} are errors.

Assuming that the error structure is $E(\epsilon_{it}) = 0$, $E(\epsilon_{it}^2) = \sigma^2$, and $E(\epsilon_{it}\epsilon_{jt}) = 0$ for $i \neq j$, Equation 3.1 is a fixed effects model. The β capture the effects of the macroeconomic variables on all individuals, and the α_i capture the effects peculiar to individual i over all time (Hsiao 1986: ch. 3).

If r_{it} were observed, one could use ordinary least squares (OLS) to estimate Equation 3.1, but rather than r_{it}, we observe discrete votes, r_{it}^*, defined by:

$$r_{it}^* = 1 \quad if\, r_{it} > r_t \tag{3.2}$$

$$r_{it}^* = 0 \quad if\, r_{it} \leq r_t \tag{3.3}$$

where "1" denotes a vote for tighter policy, and r_t is the current federal funds rate.[21]

With the definition of r_{it}^* in Equation 3.2, and the assumption that ϵ_{it} is normally distributed $(0, \sigma^2)$, Equation 3.1 is a binary probit, fixed effects model:[22]

$$P(r_{it}^* = 1) = P(r_{it} > r_t)$$
$$= \Phi(\frac{\alpha_i}{\sigma} + \frac{\beta' x_t}{\sigma} - \frac{r_t}{\sigma}) \tag{3.4}$$

A nonstandard aspect of this equation is its relationship to contingent valuation models that are often used to estimate the willingness to pay for environmental quality (Cameron and Huppert 1991). In effect r_t is a referendum question. At time t, each FOMC member receives a

---

[21] The coding of the data is binary due to limitations in the voting data. See data section for more details.

[22] We can also entertain other distributional assumptions. I assume the normal for convenience. The resulting estimation of the probit model is relatively simple, and the estimates are consistent for large T.

take-it-or-leave-it question based on the current interest rate: Do you find a higher interest rate acceptable compared to the current interest rate? If the answer is "yes", $r_{it}^* = 1$, and if the answer is "no", $r_{it}^* = 0$.

The parameters of the model are easy to estimate with any standard package. I used SST version 4.0. According to Hsiao (1986: 159), the maximum likelihood estimates of the parameters are consistent when the number of observations per individual is large – as is the case in my dataset (see Section 3.3).

3.2.3 The α_is as Ideal Point Estimates

Note that in Equations 3.1, 3.2, and 3.4, references are to r_{it} – the individual's ideal point at time t. But as explained previously, we need r_i, the ideal point irrespective of time. As a result, we are particularly interested in the α_i coefficients, which are not dependent on time, as proxies for r_i. From Equation 3.4, since:[23]

$$\frac{\partial P(r_{it}^* = 1)}{\partial \alpha_i} = \phi(\alpha_i + \beta' x_t - r_t)$$
$$> 0 \tag{3.5}$$

the higher the value of α_i, the greater the likelihood that individual i votes for tighter policy. Thus an individual with a high value of α_i tends to favor tighter policy, while those with lower values favor easier policy. In this manner, α_i is a proxy *time independent* estimate of the true ideal federal funds rate for individual actor i.

A legitimate question about this model is: if one is interested in individual characteristic variables, why not *explicitly* include them in the model as variables in their own right? The reasons are twofold. First, it can be difficult to identify and/or measure these variables. Many individual-specific variables potentially affect ideal points including party affiliation, profession, years in government, and level of education, but identifying the complete and relevant set of variables is not necessarily possible. In terms of measurement, education, for example, can be measured by tangibles such as level, type, and number of degrees, but other more intangible features, such as the conservativeness of the education, are more difficult to measure.

---

[23] Henceforth, for notational simplicity, I drop σ from the equations. Normalizing σ to one just changes the scaling of the estimates.

Table 3.2: *Summary Characteristics of the Data*

	FOMC	Senate Banking Committee	President	Macroeconomic Variables
Period	1970–95	1974–95	1969–94	1969–95
Frequency	every 6 weeks	every 6 months	monthly	monthly
No. of observations	2966	660	305	324
$y_{it} = 1$	47.70%	39.90%	39.70%	
$y_{it} = 0$	52.30%	60.60%	60.30%	

Second, the particular variables themselves are not always of interest per se. Rather, an estimate of general individual characteristics is more important for some applications. In testing the appointment process model, we want to know where individual ideal points lie relative to one another – not necessarily why individuals have a particular ideal point. The α_i estimates are single measures of all the individual-specific characteristics that inform us of the relative location of the actors.

3.3 DATA, ESTIMATED MODEL, AND RESULTS

3.3.1 The Data

The estimation uses two new datasets of FOMC voting and Senate Banking Committee signals, and two existing datasets for the presidents and economic variables.

1. The FOMC Voting Data (Table 3.2). This dataset is a panel of each FOMC member's vote (for tighter or easier policy) at the approximately monthly meetings during the period 1970–95.

I constructed this dataset by analyzing the formal voting records contained in the *Federal Reserve Bulletin*'s "The Record of Policy Actions." The coding involved a two-step process. First, I assigned a direction, tighter or easier, to each meeting's "Current Economic Policy" or "Domestic Policy Directive."[24] When the FOMC decided to maintain prevailing conditions,

---

[24] A binary rather than a three-level variable is used because individuals rarely truly vote for the status quo. When the FOMC votes for the status quo, they almost always assign a tight or easy bias to their vote. Due to the high percentage of votes in which some bias is mentioned, it was quite difficult to confidently code status quo votes as real status quo votes.

I assigned a direction based on that of the previous meeting. Second, I assigned the directive's direction to each member in the directive's voting majority. For each member in the minority, I assigned a direction based on explicit references to the direction she would have preferred. In contrast to many previous studies,[25] this study includes all votes at meetings, nondissents as well as dissents, and therefore utilizes all the information contained in the formal voting records.

The entire dataset also contains data from 1951–69, but I did not use that data because the FOMC used a different set of criteria for judging economic conditions during that period. Beck (1982a: 420, 422) points out that before 1970, the FOMC under Chairman Martin did not rely on quantitative economic indicators, preferring to rely instead on the "tone" of markets. According to Maisel (1973: 114), a former Fed member, "[Martin] felt that the economy was too complex to explain in detail; intuition would be lost and false leads followed if too much stress were put on measurement," and (1973: 118) "[Martin] pointed out again and again the inability of everyone, including himself, to explain movements in the money supply – a fact which led him to put his faith in the tone and feel of financial markets as opposed to specific measurements." Essentially the Fed's consistent reliance on econometric modeling of the economy came only after Martin left the chairman's office. Thus for consistency in the data, I stuck to the post-Martin period.

In the estimation for 1970–95, there were seventy-two FOMC members and 258 FOMC meetings. I could not estimate the α_i parameter for individuals who voted in one direction 100 percent of the time because the α_i estimates for such individuals tended to infinity. However, in the next chapter's empirical analysis of the model's predictions, I do include these individuals in the rank orderings of the contemporaneous FOMC members by placing them on the extreme ends of the distribution; thus an individual who voted for tight policy 100 percent of the time was placed at the tightest position of the twelve FOMC members in a given period. I used an average of 42 votes per individual with a minimum of 5 (for 2 individuals) and a maximum of 137.

2. *The Senate Banking Committee Signaling Data.* This dataset consists of each Banking Committee member's (forty-two total senators) signal for tighter or easier policy relative to current FOMC policy. The signals come

---

[25] Yohe (1966); Canterbery (1967); Puckett (1984); Belden (1989); Havrilesky and Schweitzer (1990); Havrilesky and Gildea (1992).

from the semiannual monetary policy hearings (forty-three total hearings), the Humphrey-Hawkins testimonies, mandated by the Full Employment and Balanced Growth Act of 1978.[26] These hearings were meant to give the senators and the public a chance to question the Fed chairman about the Fed's current and future policy.

I analyzed statements from the testimonies during the period 1974–95. For each senator who spoke at the hearings, I coded her statement(s) in the direction appropriate to her voiced concerns. For senators who did not speak,[27] I assigned a direction based on that of the current FOMC policy. For each senator, there was an average of fifteen signals with a minimum of five and a maximum of thirty-eight.

Because the senators' remarks during the hearings are in relation to current FOMC policy, the information from these hearings is ideally suited for the estimation of the senators' and FOMC members' preferences on one common scale.

3. *The Presidential Signaling Data.* This dataset consists of each president's (six total presidents) monthly signal for tighter or easier policy from Thomas Havrilesky's SAFER dataset.[28] Havrilesky and his research assistants coded *The Wall Street Journal*'s articles that commented on the administration's stance on current FOMC policy. Thus, like the Senate data, these data consist of the president's position on FOMC policy and are ideally suited for estimating preferences for the president and FOMC members on one common scale.

For my dataset, I aggregated Havrilesky's measure on a monthly basis for the period 1969–94 (305 months) (Havrilesky 1988, 1991, 1993,

[26] The Full Employment and Balanced Growth Act of 1978 requires the Fed chairman to testify before the Senate Committee on Banking and Urban Affairs on a semiannual basis. During the period 1974–8, the act was considered in a number of different forms, and the hearings, which were to become law according to the act, began during this period. The exact titles and dates of the hearings are: 2-6-74 Oversight on Economic Stabilization, Subcommittee On Production and Stabilization; 2-25-75 Monetary Policy Oversight; 1975–1976 First thru Fourth Meetings on the Conduct of Monetary Policy, House Concurrent Resolution 133; 1977–1978 First thru Third Meetings on the Conduct of Monetary Policy, House Concurrent Resolution 133 and Public Law 95-188; 1979–1995 Federal Reserve's [First or Second] Monetary Policy Report for [Year]; and Full Employment and Balanced Growth Act of 1978 (Humphrey-Hawkins), Semiannual hearings [Feb., July].

[27] Over the entire period, 1974–94, roughly half of the Senate Banking Committee members spoke during the Humphrey-Hawkins testimonies. Fewer tended to speak during the earlier hearings, and greater numbers tended to speak in the more recent hearings.

[28] For more on this dataset, see Havrilesky 1991, 1993, and 1995.

1995). The original coding was three-tiered: easier (+1), tighter (−1), or no change (0). I summed the signals for each month. For sums greater than zero, I assigned an easy policy signal for the month. For sums less than zero, I assumed that the administration was satisfied with current FOMC policy and assigned a direction according to that of current FOMC policy. For each president, there was an average of fifty-one signals with a minimum of seventeen and a maximum of ninety-six.

4. *Macroeconomic Data.* The macroeconomic data are monthly observations of seven variables during 1970–95. The data originate from the Business Cycle Indicators (BCI) and Business Statistics (BS) historical data series produced by the U.S. Department of Commerce Bureau of Economic Analysis.

The seven variables constitute the main economic conditions to which FOMC members may be thought to respond.[29] First, the real federal funds rate, $RFFR_t$, provides the status quo policy. I define the $RFFR_t$ as the federal funds rate less the annual rate of inflation. Second, the inflation rate is the most commonly cited reason for Fed actions. I used two measures of inflation: the rate of change of the consumer price index (CPI) for inflation of consumer goods prices, and the rate of change of the prices of industrial commodities (PIC) for inflation of nonconsumer goods prices. Third, the Full Employment and Balanced Growth Act of 1978 mandates Fed attention to the unemployment rate. Fourth, the nominal effective exchange rate of the dollar captures international considerations. Fifth, the index of industrial production (IIP) is a measure of output. Finally, M1 captures direct fluctuations in the money supply.

3.3.2 The Estimated Model

I combined the three sets of data into a single matrix with 120 individuals and 312 months. With an average of forty-two votes per FOMC member,

---

[29] A more commonly used model of Fed behavior is the Taylor Rule, developed by economist John Taylor (Taylor 1993). The Taylor Rule is an optimal model of aggregate Fed behavior and states that the federal funds rate should increase in response to a rise in: (1) the difference between potential and real GDP and (2) the difference between the inflation rate and the target inflation rate of 2 percent. Taylor purposely chose a simple rule that explicitly took into account output growth and inflation. Although the Taylor Rule is based on the actual behavior of the Fed, it is largely a normative instrument that prescribes how the Fed should act (a disadvantage for my project because I am more interested in a positive analysis of the Fed's actions).

fifteen signals per senator, and fifty-one signals per president, I faced the rare panel situation of many cross-sectional *and* time series observations; therefore the parameter estimates are consistent in a probit, fixed effects model (Hsiao 1986: 159).[30]

I estimated this final model from the data:

$$
\begin{aligned}
P(r_{it}^* = 1) = \Phi[\alpha_i &- \beta_1 RFFR_t + \beta_2 INFL_{t-1} + \beta_3 UNEMP_{t-1} \\
&+ \beta_4 DOLLAR_{t-1} + \beta_5 IIP_{t-1} + \beta_6 M1_{t-1} \\
&+ \beta_7 PIC_{t-1}]
\end{aligned}
\tag{3.6}
$$

in which the α_i are coefficients on dummy variables for each individual member, and all of the other variables are summarized in Table 3.3.[31]

---

[30] Maddala (1987) recommends logit for consistency when the dependent variable is categorical, but he only considers situations in which the number of cross sections is high, and the number of observations per person is low; here, the number of observations per person is also high. I also estimated the model with logit, and the coefficient estimates correlated at 0.999.

[31] The data are quite imperfect for two reasons. First, the data frequency differs in each dataset, precluding ideal comparisons of votes or signals. We would really like to observe immediate reactions of the president and Banking Committee to any FOMC decision. Unfortunately the ideal is elusive because the FOMC meets eight times a year, the Banking Committee holds monetary policy hearings twice a year, and the president signals many times a month. Consequently, some FOMC decisions receive more attention than others by the Banking Committee and the president. Second, both the Banking Committee hearings and *The Wall Street Journal* produce noisy signals. Although monetary policy is the subject of the Banking Committee hearings, the hearings often focus on fiscal policy as well. In addition, the hearings can be poorly attended. As for *The Wall Street Journal*, it faces other news constraints and may fail to report all the president's monetary policy signals. Either source may contain statements that focus on tightening moves because they are more controversial than easing moves.

Because the data exhibit variation in both frequency and reliability, one estimation model for all three sets of actors might be problematic because it would imply that the errors are drawn from the same distribution. I therefore estimated two empirical models in addition to Equation 3.6, one each for the president and Senate Banking Committee.

1. Senate Banking Committee

$$P[r_{it}^* = 1] = \Phi[\alpha_i - \beta_1 RFFR_t + \beta_2 INFL_t + \beta_3 UNEMP_{t-1} + \beta_4 IIP_{t-1}] \tag{7.1}$$

2. President

$$P[r_{it}^* = 1] = \Phi[\alpha_i - \beta_1 RFFR_t + \beta_2 INFL_t + \beta_3 UNEMP_t + \beta_4 IIP_t] \tag{7.2}$$

I calculated the correlation of the ideal point estimates from these models with those from the larger model. The ideal points of the two sets of presidents correlate at 0.985, and the ideal points of the senators correlate at 0.968. Thus there is

Table 3.3: *Definitions of the Variables*

r_{it}	Direction of vote for member i at time t. 1 indicates a higher desired federal funds rate than the prevailing rate or tighter policy, and 0 indicates lower desired federal funds rate or easier policy.
$RFFR_t$	The real federal funds rate at time t. $RFFR_t = FFR_t$ - inflation rate. The inflation rate in this instance is the annual inflation rate calculated from the percent change of the Consumer Price Index for all urban consumers (CPI-U) from the previous 12 months.
$INFL_t$	The inflation rate as indicated by the change in the proportion of the (CPI-U) from the previous month.
$UNEMP_t$	The unemployment rate as indicated by the change in the proportion of the unemployment level from the previous month.
$DOLLAR_t$	The value of the dollar relative to a basket of foreign currencies as indicated by the change in the proportion of the value from the previous month.
IIP_t	The value of the index of industrial production as indicated by a change in the proportion of the index from the previous month.
$M1_t$	The value of M1 as indicated by a change in the proportion of M1 from the previous month. M1 consists of currency and checkable deposits.
PIC_t	The value of the producer price index for the industrial commodities grouping as indicated by a change in the proportion of the index from the previous month.

1. The β Estimates: The Macroeconomic Variables. Table 3.4 presents the coefficient estimates for the macroeconomic variables. The overall fit is good with approximately 71 percent of the votes predicted correctly ex post. The estimates are in the predicted directions and significant at all conventional levels.

DIRECTION OF THE COEFFICIENTS. The directions of the coefficient estimates are as expected. First, inflation (INFL, PIC), growth (IIP), and money supply (M1) positively affect the probability of voting for tighter policy; essentially, the results show that the Fed tries to put a cap on an overheating economy by tightening. Second, RFFR, unemployment (UNEMP), and the dollar exchange rate (DOLLAR) negatively affect the probability of voting for tighter policy; the Fed tries to stimulate

very little difference between using the separately specified models versus the larger model.

Table 3.4: *Estimated Coefficients on the Macroeconomic Variables*

	Dependent Variable: DIR VOTE$_t$					
	(1)	(2)	(3)	(4)	(5)	(6)
RFFR$_t$	−0.0860	−0.0831	−0.0903	−0.0827	−0.0855	−0.1048
	(0.0009)	(0.0095)	(0.0097)	(0.0100)	(0.0102)	(0.0165)
INFL$_t$	0.4266	0.1410	0.1813	0.2887	0.7106	0.2559
	(0.0794)	(0.0751)	(0.0759)	(0.0784)	(0.0941)	(0.1058)
UNEMP$_{t-1}$		−0.2680	−0.2550	−0.2739	−0.3098	−0.2979
		(0.0203)	(0.0205)	(0.0212)	(0.0220)	(0.0224)
DOLLAR$_{t-1}$			−0.0464	−0.0636	−0.0621	−0.0641
			(0.0106)	(0.0109)	(0.0110)	(0.0111)
IIP$_{t-1}$				0.3938	0.41846	0.47044
				(0.0280)	(0.0289)	(0.0304)
M1$_{t-1}$					0.3768	0.4398
					(0.0455)	(0.0468)
PIC$_{t-1}$						0.4771
						(0.0467)
log L	−2558.2	−2467.5	−2458.0	−2350.9	−2315.8	−2261.1
Percent correctly predicted	64.91	67.11	67.28	69.67	70.40	70.86

Values in parentheses are standard errors

the economy through easing when the economy descends into a recession, as higher rates of unemployment would indicate. As for the exchange rate, the Fed may try to keep the dollar from running too high against other currencies, as the Fed did in the mid-80s. Regarding the RFFR, the negative sign could indicate that the FOMC moderates the RFFR by reducing its value when it increases and increasing it when it decreases.

MAGNITUDE. As in all probit models, the magnitude of the βs is not directly interpretable; for true magnitude, we need to examine the marginal effects of x_t with respect to $P(r_{it}^* = 1)$:

$$\frac{\partial P(r_{it}^* = 1)}{\partial x_{kt}} = \phi[\alpha_i + \beta_k' x_{kt}]\beta_k \tag{3.7}$$

where $k = \{1, \ldots, 7\}$ and indexes each of the macroeconomic variables including the RFFR. Table 3.5 presents the value of (3.7) for each variable in x_t when all other variables are evaluated at their mean values. If inflation doubles (a change of 100 percent) in a month, for example, an individual is approximately 10 percent more likely to vote for tighter policy.

Table 3.5: *Marginal Effects of the Macroeconomic Variables*

x_{kt}	Marginal Effects of x_{kt}
$RFFR_t$	−0.0415
$INFL_t$	0.1014
$UNEMP_{t-1}$	−0.1180
$DOLLAR_{t-1}$	−0.0254
IIP_{t-1}	0.1864
$M1_{t-1}$	0.1743
PIC_{t-1}	0.1891

The results bolster and break down some strongly held beliefs about the Fed's reactions to the economy. The Fed is often attacked for reacting too strongly to inflation and not strongly enough to unemployment, the latter being one of the impetuses for the Full Employment and Balanced Growth Act of 1978. However, the congressional draftees of the act would be pleased by these results; according to Table 3.5, the Fed reacts with nearly equal weight to both consumer inflation and unemployment, although it is also clear that the Fed reacts more strongly to inflation in terms of the PIC. The Fed is also often attacked for squelching growth; in fact, the results do indicate that the Fed tightens in response to growth and that it reacts more strongly to growth (IIP) than any other variable except for the PIC.

The Fed also responds to international considerations in the form of the nominal effective exchange rate although at a lower level compared to the domestic variables. Previous studies of FOMC behavior concluded that the FOMC does not consider international factors, which seems counter-intuitive given the Fed's active role in notable international events.[32] In contrast, this study finds significant effects of the dollar on voting prob-abilities during 1970–95. A number of important international events probably contributed to this effect, including the 1971 switch from the gold standard, the oil shocks of 1973 and 1979, and the overvaluation of the dollar in 1986. International effects could be missing from the previous

---

[32] Chappell, Havrilesky, and McGregor (1993): 197, fn. 21: "Following other reac-tion function studies, we also considered exchange rates and balance of payments measures as possible explanatory variables. Like most of those studies, we find little evidence that international variables have consistently influenced monetary policy." See also Beck (1982a) who uses the Deutsche Mark as an independent variable but finds that it is not significant (p. 426).

studies because they covered longer or shorter time periods that exclude these events.[33]

The α_i Estimates: Ideal Points. Tables 3.6, 3.7, 3.8 present the α_i estimates for the FOMC members, senators, and presidents in order of easiest to tightest policy.

The extent to which the α_i estimates are reasonable can be measured by the extent to which they tend to confirm anecdotal evidence of the monetary policy reputations. From those standards, the estimates in Tables 3.6, 3.7, and 3.8 appear quite reasonable.

In line with the scarce sources on this subject, FOMC members with reputations for easier policy, such as Maisel or Seger, tend to top the list while those with reputations for tighter policy, such as Volcker, tend toward the bottom. Burns was known as somewhat liberal but more conservative than Maisel, and Burns follows Maisel on the estimate list. Coldwell, Partee, and Wallich were known as staunch tight-policy advocates and are located near the bottom of the list. The sources consist of a few books (Maisel 1973; Greider 1987) and conversations with current and former Fed staff members.

Despite the success in locating most of the members relative to one another, some of the estimates seem off especially in the more recent FOMC sessions. Greenspan seems too liberal, and Yellen and Blinder seem much too tight. For Yellen and Blinder, the problem is that they had relatively small numbers of observations (ten for Blinder, nine for Yellen) during a period dominated by indications of overheating and therefore tightening moves by the FOMC. For others like Greenspan, the period between 1987 and the early 90s was characterized by a long period of easing by the Fed because of the 1987 stock market crash and the ensuing recession. As more data points are added to the dataset, the individuals will have greater numbers of observations that expose them to a greater variety of conditions, which in turn will allow us to pinpoint their preferences more precisely.

As for Senate members, Alfonse D'Amato, a strong critic of tight monetary policy, is near the top while Proxmire, a supporter of tight monetary policy, is near the bottom. In the Humphrey-Hawkins testimonies, D'Amato repeatedly riled against the Fed for policy that he deemed too tight. Proxmire often extolled the virtues of a tight policy FOMC and criticized the Fed for easing too much.

---

[33] Chappell, Havrilesky, and McGregor (1993, 1995) describe the period 1960–87 (p. 198). Beck (1982a) covers the period March 1970–August 1979 (p. 423).

Table 3.6: FOMC Members – Ideal Point Estimates

Member	Estimate of α	Standard Error	Member	Estimate of α	Standard Error	Member	Estimate of α	Standard Error
Swan	−0.44573	0.56759	Robertson	0.96026	0.22252	Minehan	1.41854	0.59756
Hickman	−0.10306	0.50784	Treiber	0.97277	0.44357	Jackson	1.43039	0.26516
Seger	0.01634	0.26130	LaWare	0.99017	0.23199	Eastburn	1.48211	0.28091
Johnson	0.16581	0.28284	Boykin	1.00094	0.28667	Volcker	1.50463	0.21681
Holland	0.16785	0.34706	Brimmer	1.01859	0.20796	Phillips	1.53465	0.28166
Corrigan	0.41728	0.22622	Sherrill	1.06946	0.25674	Solomon	1.57756	0.28954
Heller	0.42739	0.30968	Morris	1.07991	0.22251	Martin	1.58188	0.31276
Angell	0.46858	0.23166	Lilly	1.17698	0.32771	Gardner	1.58530	0.28774
Maisel	0.50188	0.23890	Keehn	1.18372	0.24373	Lindsey	1.62146	0.28245
Mullins	0.61680	0.30886	Winn	1.24786	0.23789	Baughman	1.62867	0.32899
Bucher	0.66585	0.28271	Kimbrel	1.24971	0.24483	Partee	1.65010	0.22469
Horn	0.67352	0.36558	Parry	1.25718	0.30125	Coldwell	1.65366	0.21881
Mitchell	0.69600	0.20878	Hoskins	1.27353	0.36238	Gramley	1.66531	0.28953
Debs	0.73775	0.75914	Clay	1.27699	0.26800	Wallich	1.75048	0.21834
Sheehan	0.74245	0.27004	Hayes	1.28455	0.21865	Roos	1.76330	0.31540
Hoenig	0.75658	0.40557	Rice	1.29466	0.25055	Yellen	1.91701	0.49707
Greenspan	0.77746	0.22052	Teeters	1.31102	0.25987	Blinder	1.97705	0.48522
MacLaury	0.82441	0.35561	Forrestal	1.34058	0.27701	Scanlon	1.97883	0.56589
Stern	0.85236	0.30648	Jordan	1.34621	0.36746	Bopp	2.07879	0.54823
Kelley	0.85711	0.21764	Guffey	1.34950	0.24591	McTeer	2.31671	0.51583
Melzer	0.87210	0.28802	Balles	1.37432	0.25764	Ford	2.40089	0.50317
Daane	0.89784	0.21293	Black	1.37598	0.23599	McDonough	2.51151	0.42555
Burns	0.89930	0.20478	Mayo	1.37898	0.22859	Timlen	2.62590	0.63862
Boehne	0.92204	0.26374	Schultz	1.40884	0.32499	Willes	2.63177	0.54602
Francis	0.95390	0.29349	Moskow	1.41854	0.59756	Roberts	2.70825	0.60184
						Miller	2.79723	0.51513

Table 3.7: *Senate Banking Committee Members – Ideal Point Estimates*

Member	Estimate of α	Standard Error	Member	Estimate of α	Standard Error	Member	Estimate of α	Standard Error
Sasser	−0.17323	0.40818	McIntyre	0.93180	0.50178	Sparkman	1.27723	0.48172
Wirth	0.33217	0.48294	Mattingly	0.93478	0.48015	Morgan	1.33903	0.44274
Roth	0.36939	0.51219	Chafee	1.01436	0.48864	Proxmire	1.36791	0.30751
Graham	0.50990	0.44288	Bond	1.03484	0.35648	Schmitt	1.37644	0.49800
Sanford	0.50990	0.44288	Shelby	1.03484	0.35648	Domenici	1.41183	0.52561
Riegle	0.53805	0.29353	Boxer	1.04153	0.57371	Armstrong	1.41209	0.34597
Dixon	0.62503	0.33621	Bryan	1.07047	0.40989	Tower	1.56822	0.34242
Sarbanes	0.71877	0.28122	Cranston	1.08312	0.28203	Gorton	1.58323	0.49676
Mack	0.81863	0.42410	Gramm	1.10088	0.32593	Helms	1.62073	0.60185
Kerry	0.82032	0.42350	Dodd	1.10660	0.29928	Bennett	1.83670	0.57963
Kassebaum	0.83164	0.45345	Hecht	1.14117	0.40510	Lugar	1.86913	0.43415
Heinz	0.86290	0.29940	Garn	1.14880	0.27973	Faircloth	2.25117	0.70224
D'Amato	0.87573	0.29902	Williams	1.22253	0.38565	Moseley-Braun	2.25117	0.70224
Brooke	0.93180	0.50178	Stevenson	1.24178	0.42616	Murray	2.25117	0.70224

Table 3.8: *Presidents – Ideal Point Estimates*

President	Estimate of α	Standard Error
Bush	−0.66979	0.37614
Nixon	0.76827	0.20731
Ford	0.95333	0.35003
Carter	1.21460	0.25732
Reagan	1.21926	0.22658
Clinton	1.93938	0.35871

The estimates for the presidents are somewhat surprising. In contrast to the preferences for fiscal policy, there is no easy conclusion regarding whether Republicans prefer one type of policy versus the Democrats. George H. W. Bush tops the list as the easiest policy advocate, while Clinton bottoms out the list as the tightest policy advocate. A mixture of Republicans and Democrats populate the middle region between these two ends. Reagan is where he should be according to Chappell, Havrilesky, and McGregor (1993) and Greider (1987); as a supply-sider, he was well known for wanting easy members on the Fed.

As far as the relationship between the dimensions of fiscal and monetary policy, it is tough to conclude that there is a clear relationship. Bush was known for his fiscal conservatism, and Reagan is known for tripling the national debt. The two are at opposite ends of the monetary policy spectrum, which implies that fiscal conservatives are easy monetary policy advocates and vice versa. However, this sort of reasoning breaks down for the Democrats. Carter was fiscally more liberal than Clinton, and yet, Carter is also more liberal in terms of monetary policy rather than more conservative. On the congressional side, Boxer and Gramm are in the middle, and Moseley-Braun is at the tight money end. Further research is definitely needed in this regard.

3.4 SUMMARY

Empirical tests of spatial models require ideal point estimates. Normally, the best data we have for estimating ideal points consist of a panel of individual votes or signals. The same individuals in these data make different choices in different contexts. In terms of monetary policy, changing economic conditions affect whether policymakers vote for tighter monetary policy. They are more likely to do so when inflation is high than during a recession. Methods of ideal point estimation that do not control for these economic conditions yield similar or identical estimates for all individuals. Vote proportions and Americans for Democratic Action (ADA) scores are two commonly used ideal point measures that suffer from this problem.

This chapter developed a method based on the fixed effects model that controls for economic conditions and produces unique ideal point estimates that are comparable across both time and institutions. As the appendix in Section 3.5 points out, the method is similar to NOMINATE but uses macroeconomic control variables as vote covariates, which provides efficiencies in the number of estimated parameters, saves estimation time, provides intuitive coefficient interpretations, and provides instant standard errors.

The method yields reasonable estimates of monetary policy preferences for all the major actors involved in monetary policy making: presidents, Senate Banking Committee members, and FOMC members. These estimates are used in the next chapter to test the implications of the appointment process model.

Although this chapter focuses on monetary policy preferences, the problems described are hardly unique to this area. The method can be used to estimate preferences over any dimension affected by economic conditions, time, and issues of comparability across institutions. Fiscal policy, stock market regulation, welfare policy, and unemployment policy are just a few of the areas in which changing economic conditions are likely to affect policy votes at a given point in time. The method can also be used to estimate preferences across time and institutions; testing any separation of powers model requires such estimates. Thus the method is applicable to a variety of ideal point estimation problems in which the contexts for voting are different across sets of individuals and are dynamically changing.

3.5 APPENDIX: A COMPARISON WITH NOMINATE

The past two decades have witnessed the increased use of spatial models in political science. A consequence of this occurrence has been the development of methods to test spatial models, particularly methods to estimate the ideal points of individuals in such models. The most prominent and widely used of these methods is NOMINATE, a set of FORTRAN codes initially developed by Keith Poole and Howard Rosenthal to estimate ideal points for members of Congress from congressional roll-call votes

(Poole and Rosenthal 1985, 1997). With Poole, McCarty later extended the code to estimate presidential ideal points (McCarty and Poole 1995).

NOMINATE is an excellent method when information about the individuals and/or the votes is unavailable or costly to obtain. In the congressional setting, for example, we may know little about what affects members' ideal points such as district characteristics. Likewise for bills, we may have little information about a bill or a series of bills; a number of appropriations bills may really be about defense spending rather than the larger fiscal picture. Despite the lack of this information, NOMINATE extracts estimates for the cutpoints between "yes" and "no" votes, individual ideal points, and the dimensionality of the bills.

Using the fixed effects setup, we can estimate a one-dimensional model comparable to NOMINATE:

$$r_{it} = \alpha_i + \beta'_t X_t + \epsilon_{it} \tag{3.8}$$

where t now indexes votes, and X_t is a vector of dummy variables for the T votes rather than the macroeconomic variables. This model therefore contains dummy variables for each individual *and* each vote. It produces N, α estimates, one for each individual, and T, β estimates, one for each vote.

The β estimates from this model and the cutpoint estimates for NOMINATE are similar although not exactly identical. First, both are vote parameters that affect the individual equally and are estimated holding individual ideal points constant. Second, the estimates of β from Equation 3.8 are effectively cutpoints. In the NOMINATE setup, individual ideal points are fixed, and cutpoints for bills move among them to determine who votes "yes" and "no" on the bill. In Equation 3.8, the cutpoint and the ordering of individual ideal points are fixed, and the coefficients move the entire individual orderings around the cutpoint. Both models use the estimates to determine the probability of an individual voting "yes" for tighter policy.

Under the right conditions, there are four advantages to using the fixed effects setup presented in the previous sections of this chapter. First, there are efficiency gains in the number of estimated parameters. In the context of FOMC votes, suppose there were fifty votes in the 1970s. With this data, NOMINATE would estimate fifty vote parameters, one cutpoint parameter for each vote. The setup in this chapter uses available information about high inflation in the 70s as a proxy for the cutpoints. As a result, only one parameter, the coefficient on the inflation rate, rather than fifty parameters, one for each vote, needs to be estimated – a savings of forty-nine estimated parameters. Suppositions aside, seven macroeconomic variables, rather than the inflation rate alone, tie down the cutpoints for the 268 FOMC votes in the period 1970–95. Compared to the NOMINATE setup, there is a savings of 261 vote parameter estimates.

Second, because the number of estimated parameters is far fewer in the fixed effects setup, the model is much faster to estimate. While it takes about one minute to estimate the probit, fixed effects model, NOMINATE can take as long as one-and-a-half hours depending on computing power. The main reason for the difference in estimation time is that the sheer number of estimated parameters is far smaller for the fixed effects model estimation – for example, for the FOMC: 268 vote parameters +72 individual parameters = 340 total for NOMINATE, and 7 macroeconomic coefficients +72 individual parameters = 79 total for the fixed effects model.

Third, the probit model structure allows for easily interpretable coefficients. With correct manipulations, each coefficient adds to or subtracts from the probability of voting for higher interest rates, and this probability is bounded between zero and one. As discussed previously in Equation 3.7 and Table 3.5, a one-unit change in the macroeconomic variables leads to a $\phi(\alpha_i + \beta' x_t - r_t)$ change in the probability of any individual voting for tighter policy. For instance, if unemployment rises by 100 percent, the probability of any FOMC member voting for tighter policy drops by approximately 10 percent. The interpretations are couched in nicely understood percentage terms.

Fourth, standard errors are easily estimated. They are simply the standard errors of the coefficients from a probit model. The standard errors of the point estimates using NOMINATE are difficult to calculate, although NOMINATE coefficients are not alone in this regard; neither the Heckman/Snyder estimates (Heckman and Snyder 1997) nor the Groseclose/Snyder estimates (Groseclose, Levitt, and Snyder 1999) have easily computed standard errors. Although standard errors may not be needed in some applications, they are certainly needed for testing spatial models like the appointment process model. As will be seen in the next chapter, to test the point prediction of a model, one needs to perform hypothesis tests of whether the point prediction and the actual point are statistically different from one another.

Thus there are real gains to be made from utilizing available information. There may be fewer parameters to estimate, faster estimation of the remaining parameters, intuitive interpretations of coefficients, and easily calculable standard errors.

But it is important to point out that the method presented here only works optimally under certain conditions. Most importantly, the dimensionality of the issue must be well known, and the direction of votes must be clearly identifiable. It is also important to identify properly useable vote covariates although the model can be estimated without the covariates. All three conditions are met in monetary policy, and it is not difficult to imagine that being the case for many other areas of economic policy such as fiscal policy. If the conditions are not met, NOMINATE is the better option because NOMINATE teases out information from the data such as the dimensionality of the issue space.

4

Empirically Testing the Model's Predictions

With the ideal point estimates from Chapter 3, this chapter tests the model's predictions from Chapter 2. For each Fed appointment opportunity, I use the ideal point estimates to order the appointing president and the Senate median among the Fed members who remain after the retiree leaves. This ordering produces a point prediction for the Fed median, which we can compare to the actual Fed median in the data.

The model is used to test two sets of hypotheses for the FOMC and the BOG. The first set of hypotheses answers the question of whether political influence on monetary policy occurs through Fed appointments. The second set concerns the question of influence by whom: the president alone or both the president and Senate. The chapter first considers these hypotheses for the FOMC and then for the BOG.

The results for both the FOMC and the BOG show that political influence occurs. On the FOMC, influence is by both the president and Senate, while on the BOG, it is unclear who influences. But because the FOMC is the more important monetary policy-making body, the results show generally that appointments are an important avenue of political influence on monetary policy by both the president and Senate rather than the president alone.

The chapter proceeds by describing the appointments data. I then restate the model's predictions and enumerate the exact procedures by which I test the predictions. Finally, I present the results in turn for the FOMC and for the BOG.

4.1 THE DATA ON APPOINTMENTS

I examine twenty-three appointments made in the period 1975–94. Table 4.1 contains complete details regarding each appointment: the

Table 4.1: *The Data on Appointments*

Appointee	Appointment Date	Start Date	President		Senate Median		FOMC Median		BOG Median	
Jackson	5/22/75	7/14/75	Ford	0.95333	Williams	1.22253	Hayes, Mayo	1.00729	Burns	0.89930
Gardner	11/15/75	2/13/76			Williams	1.22253	Eastburn, Volcker	1.19981	Gardner	1.58530
Lilly	11/15/75	6/1/76			Williams	1.22253	Black, Jackson	1.10070	Gardner	1.58530
Partee	12/5/75	1/5/76			Williams	1.22253	Jackson, Eastburn	1.14603	Gardner	1.58530
Miller	12/8/77	3/8/78	Carter	1.21460	Williams	1.22253	Gardner, Coldwell	1.26623	Partee	1.65010
Teeters	8/28/78	9/18/78			Williams	1.22253	Gardner, Coldwell	1.26623	Partee	1.65010
Rice	4/12/79	6/20/79			Stevenson	1.24178	Black	1.09879	Partee	1.65010
Schultz	4/12/79	7/27/79			Stevenson	1.24178	Black	1.09879	Partee	1.65010
Volcker	7/25/79	8/6/79			Stevenson	1.24178	Black	1.09879	Volcker	1.50463
Gramley	2/29/80	5/28/80			Williams	1.22253	Schultz, Volcker	1.15803	Volcker	1.50463
Martin	1/11/82	3/31/82	Reagan	1.21926	Dodd	1.10660	Volcker, Martin	1.26595	Martin	1.58188
Seger	5/31/84	7/2/84			Dodd	1.10660	Rice, Volcker	1.10863	Martin	1.58188
Angell	10/10/85	2/7/86			Cranston	1.08312	Melzer, Morris	0.72266	Rice	1.29466
Johnson	10/10/85	2/7/86			Cranston	1.08312	Melzer, Morris	0.72266	Rice	1.29466
Heller	5/12/86	8/19/86			Cranston	1.08312	Melzer, Horn	0.52190	Angell	0.46858
Kelley	1/21/87	5/20/87			Chaffee, Bond	1.02460	Stern	0.60990	Heller, Angell	0.44799
Greenspan	6/2/87	8/11/87			Chaffee, Bond	1.02460	Greenspan	0.56458	Heller, Angell	0.44799
LaWare	5/23/88	8/15/88			Chaffee, Bond	1.02460	Greenspan, Kelley	0.60702	Angell	0.46858
Mullins	12/8/89	5/21/90	Bush	−0.66979	Kerry	0.82032	Greenspan, Stern	0.58724	Mullins	0.61680
Lindsey	1/14/91	11/26/91			Kerry	0.82032	Hoenig, Greenspan	0.54047	Greenspan	0.77746
Phillips	8/27/91	12/2/91			Kerry	0.82032	Hoenig, Greenspan	0.54047	Kelley	0.85711
Blinder	4/22/94	7/1/94	Clinton	1.93938	Boxer	1.04153	Forrestal	1.11935	Phillips	1.53465
Yellen	4/22/94	8/1/94			Shelby	0.52551	Forrestal, Phillips	1.20727	Phillips	1.53465

appointee's name, the appointment date, the date on which the appointee took office, the appointing president, the appointing Senate Banking Committee median, the FOMC median, and the BOG median. The numbers in the columns next to the presidents, the Senate medians, FOMC medians, and the BOG medians indicate their respective ideal point estimates.

The period covered exhibited considerable political and economic variation. On the political side, the twenty-three appointments encompassed five presidential administrations, of which three were Republican (Ford, Reagan, and Bush), and two were Democratic (Carter and Clinton). Reagan had the highest number of appointment opportunities at eight, and Clinton had the fewest number at two, although he went on to appoint four more during his two administrations. The appointments also encompassed at least ten different Senate Banking Committees with four different chairs – Proxmire, Garn, Riegle, and D'Amato.

The economic conditions also varied considerably. The period started in the 70s with hyperinflation and stagflation. There were recessions in the late 70s, early 80s, and early 90s as well as booms in the mid- to late 80s and mid-90s. The stock market exhibited similar trends during this period culminating in the 1987 crash.

The changing political and economic landscape meant that the Fed faced considerable challenges during this period. The 70s were characterized by a phenomenon unknown until then – stagflation, a period of high inflation and low growth. Some blame Arthur Burns, the Fed chair until 1977, for insufficient vigilance toward inflation during the early to mid-70s. The Fed certainly lost some credibility just before the 1972 election when Burns was accused of backing down to political pressures from the president. Miller, the next chair, was widely criticized for his inability to solve the economy's problems and particularly for the Fed's continual unexpected behavior. By the time Miller left in 1979, the economy was in deep trouble, and the Fed's reputation had taken a beating. In fact, for the first time in forty-two years, Congress took serious legislative actions with regard to the Fed in the Full Employment and Balanced Growth Act of 1978 that mandated Fed attention to unemployment and hearings before congressional committees.

Carter brought in Volcker to remedy both the problem of stagflation and the Fed's reputation. Volcker immediately and consistently raised rates to very high levels, which proved to be an unpopular set of moves. For example, near the beginning of his term, home building contractors protested the sharp rate hikes (Greider 1987: 189). Despite the protests, Volcker stuck to his guns, and he is widely credited for ending hyperinflation and stagflation during the 80s as well as resurrecting the Fed's reputation.

However, Volcker stayed a hawk too long against a president and Congress who were decidedly more dovish. When Volcker continued to insist on maintaining high rates in the mid 80s, he was at one point outnumbered on a vote by recent Reagan appointees. This event was unprecedented; no chair had ever lost a Fed vote. When it was clear that Volcker no longer had support either within the Fed or from the president or Congress, he resigned in mid-1987 (Greider 1987: 711–13).

Almost immediately after Greenspan took office in August of 1987, the stock market crashed in October. Unlike the Fed during the 1929 crash, this Fed immediately eased policy, and the market recovered slowly. Greenspan is often credited with leading the economy out of the ensuing crisis and recession. Like Volcker's Fed, Greenspan's Fed has often made unpopular rate hikes such as in 1991 and 1994, but probably not to the same extent as Volcker's Fed.

Thus much happened during the period under study both for the Fed and the context in which it functioned. The model from Chapter 2 looks at how some of this context influenced the Fed – namely political changes in the presidency and Congress and their policy repurcussions through appointments. We now turn to how well the model's predictions are empirically supported.

4.2 THE PROCEDURES FOR TESTING THE MODEL

In the discussion of the appointment process model in Chapter 2, *SQ2* is the theoretical model's prediction of the FOMC median for a given appointment opportunity. We now have to distinguish between this predicted FOMC median and the actual FOMC median.

Predicted versus actual. Define *PRED* as the model's predicted FOMC median, and *ACTUAL* as the actual, empirical FOMC median after an appointee takes office.

The goal of the testing procedures is to compare predicted versus actual FOMC medians, that is to test *PRED* = *ACTUAL*, for the set of twenty-three Fed appointments. In order to do so, it is necessary to identify values of the quantities, *PRED* and *ACTUAL*, for every appointment opportunity.

4.2.1 Identifying PRED

For each of the twenty-three appointment opportunities, I use the following procedures to determine *PRED*:

Step 1: Range of possible outcomes and SQ points. First, I identify the retiree, y, and the date of retirement. Second, using the retirement date, I identify and use the FOMC estimates to order the Fed members before and after the retirement.[34] This identifies the Fed median before retirement ($SQ0$), the Fed median after retirement ($SQ1$), the retiree's seat number, and the corresponding range of possible outcomes (Range 1, 2, 3, or 4 for the FOMC and Range 1, 2, or 3 for the BOG).

Step 2: Case and RR equilibrium policy. I find the president and Senate median[35] for the appointment opportunity and compare them to $SQ1$. The comparison pins down the case (1, 2, or 3) and its corresponding prediction of the RR equilibrium policy.

Step 3: PRED. I combine the range of possible outcomes with the case and RR equilibrium policy which subsequently nails down the exact prediction for the FOMC median, *PRED*, after the new appointee takes office. *PRED* is the RR equilibrium policy if it is in $[L, H]$, or otherwise, either of L or H.

Essentially the president and Senate strive to get as close as possible to the RR equilibrium policy given that the range of outcomes places constraints on the proximity with which they can reach the RR equilibrium policy. If the RR equilibrium policy is within the range of possible outcomes for a given appointment, it is the predicted policy outcome for that appointment. Otherwise, one of the upper or lower bounds of the range will be the predicted policy outcome.

The following table (Table 4.2) provides a guide for the predictions, *PRED*. The rows contain the three cases: Case 1 – presidential dominance, Case 2 – presidential compromise, and Case 3 – deadlock. As in Chapter 2, I have split Case 2 into two subcases. In the first, S is closer to P, and the RR equilibrium policy is P. In the second, S is closer to $SQ1$, and the RR equilibrium policy is SQ^-. The columns of Table 4.2 indicate whether P

---

[34] The ordering is for *all* current Fed members, including those for whom an α_i estimate is not available due to their voting 100 percent in one direction. I place those members at the extremes of the ordering.

[35] Just as I did for the Fed, I order all current senators including those who voted 100 percent in one direction.

Table 4.2: *Table of Predictions*

	P and S < SQ1	P and S > SQ1
Case 1	P if in [L, H]	P if in [L, H]
	L otherwise	H otherwise
Case 2a	P if in [L, H]	P if in [L, H]
	L otherwise	H otherwise
Case 2b	SQ^- if in [L, H]	SQ^- if in [L, H]
	L otherwise	H otherwise
Case 3	SQ1	

Entries are the values of *PRED*.

and S are to the left or right of $SQ1$. The first line of each entry indicates the *PRED* outcome if the RR equilibrium policy is in the range of possible outcomes ($\in [L, H]$), and the second line indicates the *PRED* outcome otherwise. For Case 3, the predicted outcome is always $SQ1$.

4.2.2 *Identifying ACTUAL*

I use two measures of *ACTUAL*. The first is the median of the twelve FOMC members' ideal points after the appointee took office. I designate this median as $ACTUAL_1$.

The second is the mean of a set of 1,000 simulated medians. For each FOMC, there are twelve members, each of whom has a normal ideal point distribution with mean, α_i, and a standard deviation, σ_{α_i}. For each FOMC after an appointee took office, I draw once from each of the twelve member distributions and find the median value, m, of the realized ideal points. I then conduct 1,000 sets of such draws which produces 1,000 medians. I define $ACTUAL_2$ as the mean of the 1,000 medians: $ACTUAL_2 = \mu_m = \frac{\sum_{n=1}^{1,000} m}{1,000}$.

$ACTUAL_2$ is a better measure for testing the model's predictions because it more closely reflects the true distribution of the FOMC median which is a function of twelve distributions – one for each FOMC member. In contrast, $ACTUAL_1$ only reflects the ideal point distribution of one member – the median member. Nevertheless $ACTUAL_1$ turns out to be a good approximation of the true median; the median of the twelve drawn points for any given draw is often close in value to $ACTUAL_1$. In fact, the values of $ACTUAL_2$ are not very different from those of $ACTUAL_1$; for the FOMC, the correlation between the two is 0.980, and for the BOG, it is 0.984. The real difference is in the standard deviation which is smaller for $ACTUAL_2$ than for $ACTUAL_1$, because individuals are more likely to vary than the median of those individuals; this is because the distribution of a median is generally very stable.

4.2.3 Comparing PRED to ACTUAL

In the following sections, I directly compare PRED to both $ACTUAL_1$ and $ACTUAL_2$. More precisely, I test the following hypotheses for each of the twenty-three appointments:

$$H_0 : PRED = ACTUAL \qquad (4.1)$$

$$H_a : PRED > ACTUAL \ or \ PRED < ACTUAL \qquad (4.2)$$

Thus if the model is correct and politicians do influence policy through a particular appointment, then $PRED = ACTUAL$, and we should fail to reject the null hypothesis. I therefore had to be careful about biasing the test results toward accepting the null.

I use the standard z test to test the hypotheses. Both PRED and $ACTUAL_1$ are ideal point estimates that are distributed $N(\alpha_i, \sigma_{\alpha_i})$. As for $ACTUAL_2$, the simulated distributions of the medians are also approximately normal with mean, μ_m and standard deviation, σ_m.

In the comparison of PRED and $ACTUAL_1$, I compare ideal points and use the standard errors of the ideal points in the z-statistic for the hypothesis tests. More precisely, I calculate the following z-statistic that uses the standard errors of both PRED and $ACTUAL_1$: $z = \frac{PRED-ACTUAL_1}{\sigma_{PRED-ACTUAL_1}}$ where $\sigma_{PRED-ACTUAL_1} = \sqrt{\sigma_{PRED}^2 + \sigma_{ACTUAL_1}^2 - 2COV(PRED, ACTUAL_1)}$. The estimates of σ_{PRED}^2, $\sigma_{ACTUAL_1}^2$, and $COV(PRED, ACTUAL_1)$ are available from the estimation of the ideal points.

In the comparison of PRED and $ACTUAL_2$, I compare an ideal point, PRED, to the mean of the distribution of the medians. Unlike in the comparison of PRED and $ACTUAL_1$, it would not make sense to use σ_{PRED} and σ_m in the z-statistic because both are calculated from very different methods. It would make more sense to find σ_{PRED} through means similar to those for σ_m.

However, I cannot reasonably simulate the distribution of the predicted medians due to a limitation of the theoretical model. The model does not provide precise enough predictions of the appointee's location, that is the appointee's specific α_i and σ_{α_i}. The model only specifies a range in which the appointee may be placed in order to reach the desired FOMC median. In that range, multiple combinations of α_i and σ_{α_i} may result in the same FOMC median. Without assuming an arbitrarily exact mean and standard deviation for the appointee, I was unable to run the simulations as I did for $ACTUAL_2$.

Thus I compare $ACTUAL_2$ to the fixed quantity $PRED$. As will become clear soon, treating $PRED$ as a constant biases the results against the predictions of my formal model. In addition, because $ACTUAL_1$ and $ACTUAL_2$ are close to one another, it is likely that $PRED$ and the simulated $PRED$ would also be similar.

The comparisons of $PRED$ to both $ACTUAL$s are an attempt to get at the true tests. Neither set of tests is perfect, but the truth does lie somewhere between them. On the one hand, comparing $PRED$ to $ACTUAL_1$ biases the results in the model's favor. In each case, both $PRED$ and $ACTUAL_1$ are the ideal point estimates of the median member, and each estimate has a standard error that is likely to be larger than the standard deviation of the median's true distribution, because individuals tend to vary more than the median of the individuals. Thus the z-statistic, $\frac{PRED-ACTUAL_1}{\sigma_{PRED-ACTUAL_1}}$, has a relatively large denominator that tends to push the z-statistic down and leads to more acceptances of the null than warranted. This method basically rewards large estimation errors.

On the other hand, comparing $PRED$ to $ACTUAL_2$ biases the results *against* the model. Because it is not possible to simulate a distribution for $PRED$ similar to that for $ACTUAL_2$, I compare the value of $PRED$ without its standard error to $ACTUAL_2$. The z-statistic is thus $\frac{PRED-ACTUAL_2}{\sigma_{ACTUAL_2}}$. Without the standard error of $PRED$ in the denominator, and a comparable estimated statistic, σ_{PRED}, should be in the denominator, the z-statistic is artificially large, which leads to more rejections of the null than there should be.

Therefore, the true results are somewhere between these two sets of results – one of which favors the model's predictions, and the other of which works against the model's predictions. The testing strategy is to find both sets of p-values and examine the range of p-values between the two sets. The range should give us a sense of whether or not we should accept the null hypotheses.

4.3 HYPOTHESIS TESTS – FOMC

4.3.1 *Hypothesis Tests 1: Political Influence on Monetary Policy?*

The first hypothesis corresponds to the first main question – whether politicians influence monetary policy through appointments to the Fed. As a first cut, Figure 4.1 presents a graph of the president's ideal point, the

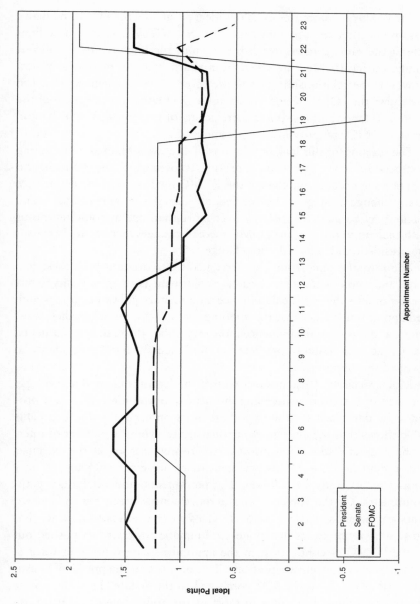

Figure 4.1: Graph of President, Senate, and FOMC Ideal Points

Senate Banking Committee median's ideal point, and the FOMC median's ideal point after the appointee took office ($ACTUAL_1$). The three lines exhibit the same general trend: higher until the late 70s, then a dip or plunge during the 80s, followed by a sharp increase in the early 90s. However, the relationship among the three is not particularly clear; in particular, the FOMC seems to vary more than either the president or the Senate. In fact, the ideal point correlations of the president/FOMC and Senate/FOMC are fairly low: 0.518 and 0.484.

The reasons for this lack of relationship are twofold. First, the rotating memberships of the reserve bank presidents, over which the president and Senate have no control, change the FOMC median even in the absence of any change in the president or Senate. Second, the same president and Senate may bargain successively over more than one appointment; thus with each appointment, the FOMC median changes incrementally even if the president and Senate do not change.

The formal model from Chapter 2 takes into account both these features, and its predictions set up each appointment as an opportunity to test the hypothesis that political influence on monetary policy occurs through Fed appointments. Because the appointment process model predicts how, when, and if politicians influence monetary policy through appointments, every match of actual to predicted FOMC median change is evidence in favor of this hypothesis.

More precisely, I use a z-test to test the hypothesis in Equation 4.1 for each of the twenty-three appointment opportunities. Table 4.3 provides the data used for the hypothesis tests on each appointment. This table shows that the appointments themselves exhibit a number of interesting characteristics. First, most of the retirements are at the extremes rather than near the FOMC median; there are nineteen Range 1 or 4 appointments, only four Range 2 appointments, and no Range 3 appointments. Of the Range 1 and 4 retirements, fifteen are in the two seats on the ends (1, 2, 11, and 12). This pattern seems to indicate that those who retire are at the fringes and may be frustrated or pushed out of the FOMC. Second, most of the appointments are made in Case 2: presidential compromise situations. This means that the president is usually farther out from the $SQ1$ compared to the Senate. Thus the Senate exerts its maximum leverage in most of the appointments. Third, both the president and Senate are out of the range of possible outcomes for the vast majority of appointments (nineteen of twenty-three). In other words, the president and Senate are relatively far from the current policy point.

Table 4.3: FOMC Hypothesis Tests 1, Data for the Hypothesis Tests

APPT.	RANGE	CASE	PRED	ACTUAL$_1$	ACTUAL$_2$
1	1	2	1.113	1.332	1.234
2	4	2	1.456	1.493	1.450
3	1	2	1.403	1.403	1.428
4	4	2	1.375	1.403	1.387
5	1	2	1.545	1.607	1.462
6	1	2	1.607	1.607	1.606
7	2, 4	2	1.377	1.394	1.493
8	2, 4	2	1.377	1.394	1.451
9	4	2	1.376	1.379	1.451
10	4	2	1.379	1.457	1.464
11	2	1	1.440	1.541	1.512
12	2	1	1.400	1.400	1.304
13	4	3	1.187	0.976	0.988
14	4	3	1.187	0.976	0.988
15	4	2	0.976	0.773	0.803
16	4	2	0.852	0.852	0.715
17	4	2	0.852	0.777	0.675
18	4	2	0.817	0.817	0.794
19	1	2	0.815	0.815	0.730
20	1	3	0.687	0.757	0.786
21	1	3	0.767	0.777	0.786
22	1	3	1.343	1.440	1.457
23	1	3	1.343	1.440	1.457

Table 4.4 shows the exact form of the hypothesis for each appointment along with the results of the tests. The results of the hypothesis tests strongly support the model's predictions. Using $ACTUAL_1$, we accept the null in twenty-one of twenty-three cases (91 percent) at the standard $\alpha = 0.10$ level. This is relatively conservative because higher levels of α make it more difficult to accept the null. Even using $ACTUAL_2$, which biases the results against the model, the p-values indicate that we accept the null for twenty out of twenty-three cases (87 percent) at the $\alpha = 0.10$ level. At lower standard α levels (e.g., $\alpha = 0.05$ or $\alpha = 0.01$), all twenty-three predicted values match the actual values using either $ACTUAL_1$ or $ACTUAL_2$. Recall that the true results lie somewhere between the results using $ACTUAL_1$ and $ACTUAL_2$. Thus *at worst* the model predicts 87 percent of the cases and *at best*, 91 percent of the cases at the $\alpha = 0.10$ level.

Regression results make the case strongly as well. Recall that the correlations of president/FOMC and Senate/FOMC are quite low, and that

Table 4.4: *FOMC Hypothesis Tests 1, Results*

APPT.	NULL	ALTERNATIVE	z	p	ACCEPT NULL?[a]	NULL	ALTERNATIVE	z	p	ACCEPT NULL?[a]
			ACTUAL$_1$					ACTUAL$_2$		
1	P <= A	P > A	0.587	0.278	yes	P <= A	P > A	1.029	0.152	yes
2	P <= A	P > A	0.263	0.396	yes	P >= A	P < A	−0.057	0.477	yes
3					yes	P <= A	P > A	0.271	0.393	yes
4	P <= A	P > A	0.203	0.419	yes	P <= A	P > A	0.106	0.458	yes
5	P <= A	P > A	0.410	0.341	yes	P >= A	P < A	−0.691	0.245	yes
6					yes	P >= A	P < A	−0.032	0.496	yes
7	P <= A	P > A	0.107	0.458	yes	P <= A	P > A	1.192	0.117	yes
8	P <= A	P > A	0.107	0.458	yes	P <= A	P > A	0.746	0.228	yes
9	P <= A	P > A	0.013	0.495	yes	P <= A	P > A	0.756	0.225	yes
10	P <= A	P > A	0.744	0.229	yes	P <= A	P > A	0.903	0.183	yes
11	P <= A	P > A	0.763	0.223	yes	P <= A	P > A	0.728	0.233	yes
12					yes	P >= A	P < A	−0.784	0.217	yes
13	P >= A	P < A	−1.434	0.076	no	P >= A	P < A	−1.458	0.072	no
14	P >= A	P < A	−1.434	0.076	no	P >= A	P < A	−1.458	0.072	no
15	P >= A	P < A	−1.155	0.124	yes	P >= A	P < A	−1.241	0.107	yes
16					yes	P >= A	P < A	−1.000	0.159	yes
17	P >= A	P < A	−0.241	0.405	yes	P >= A	P < A	−1.448	0.074	no
18					yes	P >= A	P < A	−0.200	0.421	yes
19					yes	P >= A	P < A	−0.791	0.214	yes
20	P <= A	P > A	0.254	0.400	yes	P <= A	P > A	0.787	0.216	yes
21	P <= A	P > A	0.041	0.483	yes	P <= A	P > A	0.152	0.439	yes
22	P <= A	P > A	0.593	0.277	yes	P <= A	P > A	0.789	0.215	yes
23	P <= A	P > A	0.593	0.277	yes	P <= A	P > A	0.789	0.215	yes
					21					20

[a] At the 0.10 level

Figure 4.1 shows no discernible relationships among the three sets of ideal points. In contrast, the 0.949 correlation between PRED and $ACTUAL_1$, and the 0.947 correlation between PRED and $ACTUAL_2$ indicate that the model works much better than trying to predict FOMC medians based on the separate ideal points of the appointing president and Senate median. The graph in Figure 4.2 shows this more clearly. Note the marked difference between Figures 4.1 and 4.2.

More rigorously, I tested how well PRED, the model's predictions, does versus the president and Senate's ideal points in predicting ACTUAL:

$$H_0 : ACTUAL_i = \beta_0 + \beta_1 PRED_i + \epsilon_i \tag{4.3}$$

$$H_a : ACTUAL_i = \beta_0 + \beta_1 PRES_i + \beta_2 SEN_i + \epsilon_i \tag{4.4}$$

where PRES and SEN are respectively the ideal points of the president and Senate median.

The regression results for both equations are in Table 4.5. As for which values of ACTUAL, I used $ACTUAL_2$ rather than $ACTUAL_1$ for all of the regression results in this chapter. The results with $ACTUAL_1$ are virtually identical because the two variables are very close in value.

The Cox test statistic of 1.247 with a p-value of 0.106 and the J test statistic of -1.377 with a p-value of 0.084 indicate that we accept the null at up to the $\alpha = 0.05$ level and almost the $\alpha = 0.10$ level.[36] Reversing the hypotheses with the PRES and SEN model as the null and the PRED model as the alternative, the results are even more clear-cut: the Cox test statistic is -16.68, and the J test statistic is 10.39. Thus we can reject the null in favor of the alternative, the PRED model.

Thus the evidence – both direct hypothesis tests and regressions – strongly favors the model's predictions. Politicians can instrumentally affect policy through appointments. This leaves the question of influence by whom.

4.3.2 Hypothesis Tests 2: Who Influences?

The results from the last section support the existence of political influence on the Fed through appointments, thereby answering the book's first main question. But they also partially answer the book's second question of who influences: the answer being both the president and Senate. Because the appointment process model is a model of presidential anticipation,

---

[36] See Greene (1993: 224) for details regarding the calculation of these statistics. The p-values for both test statistics come from the standard normal table.

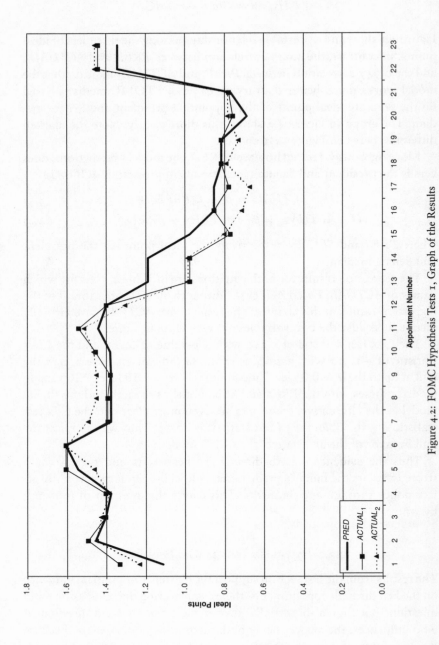

Figure 4.2: FOMC Hypothesis Tests 1, Graph of the Results

Table 4.5: *FOMC Hypothesis Tests 1, Regression Results*

Dependent Variable: $ACTUAL_2$		
	Coefficient	Coefficient
C	0.330	−0.147
	(−1.91)	(−11.27)
PRES	0.188	
	(−9.22)	
SEN	0.627	
	(−1.11)	
PRED		1.113
		(1.37)
Number of Observations	23	23
R-squared	0.369	0.897
Corrected R-squared	0.306	0.892
Sum of Squared Residuals	1.510	0.247
Standard Error of the Regression	0.275	0.109

t-statistics for H_0: $\beta = 1$ are in parentheses; for the model to be true, it is best to accept the null.

support for the model constitutes support for the influence on the Fed of both the president and Senate – if the influence is through the mechanisms of the presidential anticipation model.

However, the previous direct hypothesis tests do not indicate who exactly influences the Fed if it is not *both* the president and the Senate through the exact mechanisms of the model. The alternative hypothesis is that the entire model of presidential anticipation does not work, but this test does not show what indeed does work if the presidential anticipation model does not work. The Cox and J tests were more precise in this regard. Basically they test the model's predictions against an alternative model in which the president's and Senate's ideal points separately affect the FOMC median.

In terms of the question of who influences, it would be better to be still more precise. We would like to know that holding everything else constant, does the president *fail* to anticipate the Senate, and if so, does the president dominate the process? We could also test whether the Senate dominates the process, but I do not know of anyone who argues for Senate dominance of the appointment process. This is logical given the nature of the constitutional process that grants substantial power to the president – the power to appoint – and less power to the Senate – the power to block appointments. It is difficult to argue that the Senate dominates, and

Table 4.6: *FOMC Hypothesis Tests 2, Data for the Hypothesis Tests*

APPOINTMENT	RANGE	PRED	ACTUAL$_1$	ACTUAL$_2$
1	1	1.092	1.332	1.234
2	4	1.456	1.493	1.450
3	1	1.403	1.403	1.428
4	4	1.375	1.403	1.387
5	1	1.545	1.607	1.462
6	1	1.607	1.607	1.606
7	2, 4	1.377	1.394	1.493
8	2, 4	1.377	1.394	1.451
9	4	1.376	1.379	1.451
10	4	1.379	1.457	1.464
11	2	1.440	1.541	1.512
12	2	1.400	1.400	1.304
13	4	1.219	0.976	0.988
14	4	1.219	0.976	0.988
15	4	0.976	0.773	0.803
16	4	0.852	0.852	0.715
17	4	0.852	0.777	0.675
18	4	0.817	0.817	0.794
19	1	0.815	0.815	0.730
20	1	0.617	0.757	0.786
21	1	0.757	0.777	0.786
22	1	1.440	1.440	1.457
23	1	1.440	1.440	1.457

the president has no power in this process.[37] For the question of who influences, as for the question of influence itself, there are both: (1) direct hypothesis tests and (2) regression results.

In terms of the direct hypotheses, we can answer these questions by assuming presidential dominance for the entire period, using the model to derive new presidential dominance predictions, testing those predictions, and comparing the results to those from testing the presidential anticipation model. The results of the direct hypothesis testing of the dominance model are presented in Table 4.7; the basic information for calculating the test statistics are in Table 4.6.

[37] For the sake of completeness, I performed a Cox and J test for Senate dominance. For the test of $H_0 : ACTUAL_i = \alpha_i + \beta_1 PRED_i + \epsilon_i$ versus $H_a : ACTUAL_i = \alpha_i + \beta_1 SEN_i + \epsilon_i$, the Cox statistic is 0.82, and the J statistic is −0.84. For the reverse hypotheses, the Cox statistic is −25.47, and the J statistic is 11.63. Thus both sets of results support the null – the presidential anticipation model.

Table 4.7: *FOMC Hypothesis Tests 2, Results*

		ACTUAL$_1$					ACTUAL$_2$			
APPT.	NULL	ALTERNATIVE	z	p	ACCEPT NULL?[a]	NULL	ALTERNATIVE	z	p	ACCEPT NULL?[a]
1	P <= A	P > A	2.245	0.012	no	P <= A	P > A	1.207	0.114	yes
2	P <= A	P > A	0.263	0.396	yes	P >= A	P < A	-0.057	0.477	yes
3					yes	P <= A	P > A	0.271	0.393	yes
4	P <= A	P > A	0.203	0.419	yes	P <= A	P > A	0.106	0.458	yes
5	P <= A	P > A	0.410	0.341	yes	P >= A	P < A	-0.691	0.245	yes
6					yes	P >= A	P < A	-0.032	0.496	yes
7	P <= A	P > A	0.107	0.458	yes	P <= A	P > A	1.192	0.117	yes
8	P <= A	P > A	0.107	0.458	yes	P <= A	P > A	0.746	0.228	yes
9	P <= A	P > A	0.013	0.495	yes	P <= A	P > A	0.756	0.225	yes
10	P <= A	P > A	0.744	0.229	yes	P <= A	P > A	0.903	0.183	yes
11	P <= A	P > A	0.763	0.223	yes	P <= A	P > A	0.728	0.233	yes
12					yes	P >= A	P < A	-0.784	0.217	yes
13	P >= A	P < A	-1.234	0.109	yes	P >= A	P < A	-1.692	0.045	no
14	P >= A	P < A	-1.234	0.109	yes	P >= A	P < A	-1.692	0.045	no
15	P >= A	P < A	-1.155	0.124	yes	P >= A	P < A	-1.241	0.107	yes
16					yes	P >= A	P < A	-1.000	0.159	yes
17	P >= A	P < A	-0.241	0.405	yes	P >= A	P < A	-1.448	0.074	no
18					yes	P >= A	P < A	-0.200	0.421	yes
19					yes	P >= A	P < A	-0.791	0.214	yes
20	P <= A	P > A	0.306	0.380	yes	P <= A	P > A	1.342	0.090	no
21	P <= A	P > A	0.051	0.480	yes	P <= A	P > A	0.232	0.408	yes
22					yes	P <= A	P > A	0.118	0.453	yes
23					yes	P <= A	P > A	0.118	0.453	yes
					22					19

[a]At the 0.10 level

75

Essentially, in the theoretical models, the differences in predictions between the presidential dominance and presidential anticipation models
are in Case 2, the presidential compromise case, and Case 3, the deadlock
case. As the name, presidential dominance, suggests, the president never
compromises in this model. In the presidential anticipation model, Case 2
yielded either the president's ideal point, P, or the Senate's indifference
point, SQ^-, as the RR equilibrium policy. In contrast, if the president
always dominates the process, SQ^- will never be the long-run policy; it
will instead always be P. In Case 3 of the presidential dominance model,
the deadlock is broken by the president; whatever he wants, he gets. Predictions from Case 1 will remain the same as previously, because it is the
case of presidential dominance.

From an examination of the appointment-by-appointment direct
hypothesis tests, it is difficult to say whether the president anticipates or
dominates the Fed appointment process. Overall presidential anticipation
predicts twenty-one cases versus twenty-two for presidential dominance
using $ACTUAL_1$ at the $\alpha = 0.10$ level. With $ACTUAL_2$, the values are
twenty-one for presidential anticipation versus nineteen for presidential
dominance.

There are sixteen overlapping predictions between the two models and
seven different predictions on appointments: 1, 13, 14, 20, 21, 22, and 23.
First, in an examination of $PRED$ versus $ACTUAL_1$, three of the seven,
appointments 1, 20, and 21, favor presidential anticipation in that the
p-values for presidential anticipation compared to those for presidential
dominance more likely indicate acceptance of the null. The other four
appointments favor presidential dominance. However, for five of the seven
appointments (1, 13, 14, 20, and 21), the predictions for anticipation and
dominance are very close to one another. For instance, in appointment 21,
the anticipation prediction is 0.767, while the dominance prediction is
0.757.

Second, the results from the direct tests of $PRED$ to $ACTUAL_2$ yield
similarly unclear conclusions. As Table 4.7 indicates, appointments 1, 13,
14, and 20 are in favor of the presidential anticipation model. However,
for four of those five appointments – 1, 13, 14, and 21 – the two models'
predictions are very close to one another, and thus the four appointments
only barely favor presidential anticipation. Of the three remaining
appointments with different predictions, appointment 20 definitely favors
presidential anticipation, while appointments 22 and 23 definitely favor
presidential dominance.

Table 4.8: *FOMC Hypothesis Tests 2, Regression Results*

Dependent Variable: $ACTUAL_2$			
	Coefficient	Coefficient	Coefficient
C	0.956	−0.147	−0.083
	(−0.42)	(−11.27)	(−10.24)
PRES	0.239		
	(−8.64)		
PRED		1.113	
		(1.37)	
PRESPRED			1.054
			(0.64)
Number of Observations	23	23	23
R-squared	0.369	0.897	0.880
Corrected R-squared	0.306	0.892	0.875
Sum of Squared Residuals	1.510	0.247	0.286
Standard Error of the Regression	0.275	0.109	0.117

t-statistics for H_0: $\beta = 1$ are in parentheses; for the model to be true, it is best to accept the null.

Thus in both sets of comparisons, given the closeness of the predictions, it is not quite clear whether the president anticipates or dominates the Fed appointment process, although there is slightly more evidence for presidential anticipation.

However, the regression results strongly favor presidential anticipation (Table 4.8). In order to test for presidential anticipation versus presidential dominance, I started with Cox and J tests of the following hypotheses:

$$H_0 : ACTUAL_i = \beta_0 + \beta_1 PRED_i + \epsilon_i \qquad (4.5)$$

$$H_a : ACTUAL_i = \beta_0 + \beta_1 PRES_i + \epsilon_i \qquad (4.6)$$

We can accept the null at α as high as 0.15: the Cox statistic is 0.976 with a *p*-value of 0.165, and the J statistic is −1.028 with a *p*-value of 0.152. In reversing the hypotheses, we can reject the null that $PRES_i$ alone best predicts $ACTUAL_i$ compared to $PRED_i$; the Cox statistic is −22.510 and the J statistic is 11.445.

But these tests do not give presidential dominance a fair shake because the dominance model in this case simply posits a relationship between movements in $ACTUAL_i$ with movements in $PRES_i$. This setup does not give dominance the benefit of a theoretical model as it does to presidential anticipation. If we do provide dominance that benefit, as we did with the direct hypothesis tests, we can test the following hypotheses:

$$H_0 : ACTUAL_i = \beta_0 + \beta_1 PRED_i + \epsilon_i \qquad (4.7)$$

$$H_a : ACTUAL_i = \beta_0 + \beta_1 PRESPRED_i + \epsilon_i \qquad (4.8)$$

where *PRESPRED* is the prediction from a presidential dominance model. Basically, for the presidential dominance model, assume that P is always the RR equilibrium policy in Chapter 2's appointment process model. Then *PRESPRED* provides the point in the range of possible outcomes that is closest to P.

The results again strongly favor presidential anticipation. It is extremely difficult to reject the null in favor of the alternative because the Cox test yields 0.403 with a p-value of 0.303, and the J test yields -0.387 with a p-value of 0.349. With a reversal of the hypotheses, the Cox test statistic is -2.046 with a p-value of 0.02, and the J test statistic is 1.827 with a p-value of 0.034, both of which indicate that we can reject the null of the *PRESPRED* model in favor of the alternative, the *PRED* model.

Thus, while the evidence is not as clear-cut as that for political influence on monetary policy, it seems on balance to favor presidential anticipation versus presidential dominance. Not only do the direct hypothesis tests slightly favor anticipation, but also the regression results strongly favor anticipation.

4.4 HYPOTHESIS TESTS – BOG

4.4.1 Hypothesis Tests 1: Political Influence on Monetary Policy?

Because the president and Senate have greater potential control of the BOG compared to the FOMC, does the model more accurately predict BOG policy compared to FOMC policy?

The BOG is composed entirely of presidential appointees while the FOMC has five additional members, the reserve bank presidents, over whom the president and Senate have no control. In the model, I assume that the president and Senate can accurately predict the timing and location of each reserve bank president.

However, if that assumption is the slightest bit off, the model will inaccurately predict the FOMC median. For instance, consider a president and Senate who wish to move the median one seat to the right of the status quo. If they fail to correctly anticipate a new bank president who

Table 4.9: *BOG Hypothesis Tests 1, Data for the Hypothesis Tests*

APPT.	RANGE	CASE	PRED	ACTUAL$_1$	ACTUAL$_2$
1	1	1	0.899	0.899	0.966
2	1	2	1.430	1.585	1.499
3	1	2	1.585	1.585	1.506
4	1	2	1.430	1.585	1.342
5	1	2	1.585	1.650	1.632
6	1	2	1.650	1.650	1.639
7	1	2	1.650	1.650	1.629
8	1	2	1.650	1.650	1.524
9	3	2	1.409	1.505	1.524
10	3	2	1.409	1.505	1.522
11	1	1	1.505	1.582	1.537
12	1	1	1.582	1.582	1.523
13	3	1	1.295	1.295	1.203
14	3	1	1.295	1.295	1.203
15	3	2	1.168	0.469	0.624
16	3	2	0.448	0.448	0.486
17	3	2	0.448	0.448	0.469
18	3	2	0.469	0.469	0.551
19	1	3	0.623	0.617	0.598
20	1	3	0.697	0.777	0.904
21	1	3	0.817	0.857	0.915
22	1	2	1.093	1.535	1.349
23	1	2	1.093	1.535	1.349

also comes in to the right of the status quo, the median will move two seats to the right rather than one seat. The prediction will then be off by the distance between the two seats.

Nevertheless the model should still accurately predict the BOG median because such mistakes about the reserve bank presidents do not affect the BOG. On the BOG, the president and Senate do not have to contend with the appointments they do not control. Moving the median by one seat really means moving it by one seat rather than potentially by two, three, or up to six seats. In contrast, on the FOMC, because of the reserve bank presidents, the median can move the other way even if the president and Senate make the correct appointment for their desired direction of change. In terms of the BOG, if the president and Senate have more control at their disposal compared to the FOMC, this model of instrumental control should better predict the results for the BOG.

In fact, the model impressively predicts the BOG median (Tables 4.9 and 4.10). First, a comparison of *PRED* to *ACTUAL*$_1$ in direct hypothesis

Table 4.10: *BOG Hypothesis Tests 1, Results*

APPT.	ACTUAL$_1$ NULL	ALTERNATIVE	z	p	ACCEPT NULL?[a]	ACTUAL$_2$ NULL	ALTERNATIVE	z	p	ACCEPT NULL?[a]
1					yes	P <= A	P > A	0.402	0.344	yes
2	P <= A	P > A	0.511	0.305	yes	P <= A	P > A	0.470	0.319	yes
3					yes	P >= A	P < A	−0.582	0.280	yes
4	P <= A	P > A	0.511	0.305	yes	P >= A	P < A	−0.493	0.311	yes
5	P <= A	P > A	0.244	0.404	yes	P <= A	P > A	0.376	0.353	yes
6					yes	P >= A	P < A	−0.093	0.463	yes
7					yes	P >= A	P < A	−0.174	0.431	yes
8					yes	P >= A	P < A	−1.048	0.147	yes
9	P <= A	P > A	0.332	0.370	yes	P <= A	P > A	0.957	0.169	yes
10	P <= A	P > A	0.332	0.370	yes	P <= A	P > A	0.894	0.186	yes
11	P <= A	P > A	0.275	0.392	yes	P <= A	P > A	0.258	0.398	yes
12					yes	P >= A	P < A	−0.437	0.331	yes
13					yes	P >= A	P < A	−0.463	0.322	yes
14					yes	P >= A	P < A	−0.463	0.322	yes
15	P >= A	P < A	−0.746	0.228	yes	P >= A	P < A	−2.676	0.004	no
16					yes	P <= A	P > A	0.248	0.402	yes
17					yes	P <= A	P > A	0.148	0.441	yes
18					yes	P <= A	P > A	0.552	0.290	yes
19	P >= A	P < A	−0.022	0.491	yes	P >= A	P < A	−0.161	0.436	yes
20	P <= A	P > A	0.519	0.302	yes	P <= A	P > A	1.428	0.077	no
21	P <= A	P > A	0.351	0.363	yes	P <= A	P > A	0.635	0.263	yes
22	P <= A	P > A	0.386	0.350	yes	P <= A	P > A	1.258	0.104	yes
23	P <= A	P > A	0.386	0.350	yes	P <= A	P > A	1.258	0.104	yes
					23					21

[a] At the 0.10 level

tests shows that predicted match actual in all twenty-three cases up to the $\alpha = 0.20$ level. Even at $\alpha = 0.30$, there is a match in twenty-two of twenty-three cases. Comparing these results to those for the FOMC, there are twenty-one matches at $\alpha = 0.20$ and fifteen matches at $\alpha = 0.30$. Thus the match of *PRED* to *ACTUAL*$_1$ is greater with respect to the BOG compared to the FOMC.

Second, a comparison of *PRED* to *ACTUAL*$_2$ reveals that predicted match actual in twenty-two of twenty-three cases up to the $\alpha = 0.05$ level, while it is all twenty-three cases for the FOMC. At $\alpha = 0.10$, there are twenty-one matches for the BOG and twenty matches for the FOMC. At $\alpha = 0.20$, there are sixteen matches for the BOG versus fifteen matches for the FOMC. While the results support the model's predictions for the BOG, in terms of whether the model does better in predicting the BOG versus the FOMC, these results are less clear-cut than those using *ACTUAL*$_1$.

As with the FOMC, the true results lie somewhere in between the comparisons of *PRED/ACTUAL*$_1$ and *PRED/ACTUAL*$_2$. At best (using *ACTUAL*$_1$) the model predicts 100 percent of cases at the $\alpha = 0.10$ level, while at worst (using *ACTUAL*$_2$), the model predicts 91 percent of the cases. Thus compared to the FOMC in which the range is 87 percent to 91 percent, the BOG predictions are better born out in the data.

The regression results (Table 4.11) also strongly support the model's predictions. As a first cut, the correlations are again high, although a bit lower than those for the FOMC: the correlation between *PRED* and *ACTUAL*$_1$ is 0.901, and the correlation between *PRED* and *ACTUAL*$_2$ is 0.924.

As before, I ran Cox and J tests for the following hypotheses:

$$H_0 : ACTUAL_i = \beta_0 + \beta_1 PRED_i + \epsilon_i \qquad (4.9)$$

$$H_a : ACTUAL_i = \beta_0 + \beta_1 PRES_i + \beta_2 SEN_i + \epsilon_i \qquad (4.10)$$

The tests support the model; they allow us to accept the null. The Cox statistic for these hypotheses is 0.814 (compared to 1.237 for the FOMC) with a *p*-value of 0.208, while the J statistic is -0.761 (-1.377 FOMC) with a *p*-value of 0.223. Reversing the hypotheses also provides support for the model with a Cox statistic of -18.599 (16.68 FOMC) and a J statistic of 9.21 (10.39 FOMC). Both allow us to reject the null of the regression model with *PRES* and *SEN* as independent variables in favor of one with only *PRED*. Compared to the FOMC, these results allow us to accept the *PRED* model with greater confidence.

Table 4.11: *BOG Hypothesis Tests 1, Regression Results*

Dependent Variable: $ACTUAL_2$		
	Coefficient	Coefficient
C	0.121	0.120
	(−1.86)	(−8.59)
PRES	0.140	
	(−7.25)	
SEN	0.867	
	(−0.29)	
PRED		0.908
		(−1.13)
Number of Observations	23	23
R-squared	0.264	0.855
Corrected R-squared	0.191	0.848
Sum of Squared Residuals	2.741	0.542
Standard Error of the Regression	0.370	0.161

t-statistics for $H_0 : \beta = 1$ are in parentheses; for the model to be true, it is best to accept the null.

The evidence thus suggests that the results for the BOG are stronger compared to the FOMC. This raises the question of whether the president and Senate really try to control the BOG rather than the FOMC. Despite the evidence, this is doubtful; most discussion of candidates revolve around their influence on monetary policy which is set by the FOMC rather than the BOG.

But it certainly does not hurt to control the BOG, whose members all sit on the FOMC. As in the model, the president and Senate probably try to the best possible extent to influence the FOMC through BOG appointments, but unlike the model's assumptions, they are not always successful due to the rotations of the bank presidents.

As for the features of the appointments (Table 4.9), there are more similarities than differences from those of the FOMC appointments. First, like the FOMC predictions, most of the retirees are in the two outside ranges, Ranges 1 and 3. However, unlike the FOMC predictions, the seat numbers are more widely distributed – nearly all seat numbers are represented in the distribution. Second, like the FOMC predictions, most of the appointments are in Case 2 situations, requiring compromise between the president and Senate. Third, like the FOMC predictions, the president and Senate are within the range of possible outcomes in only one case – Heller's appointment.

4.4.2 *Hypothesis Tests 2: Who Influences?*

Just as I did for the FOMC, I examined whether the president anticipates or dominates the Senate in the BOG appointments. I developed a
presidential dominance version of the model for the BOG and tested its
predictions in both direct hypothesis tests and regression tests.

Compared with the FOMC, the results are more ambiguous for
the BOG. First, the correlation results are virtually identical although
they favor dominance very slightly. The correlation between *PRED* and
$ACTUAL_1$ is 0.927 compared to 0.901 for anticipation; for $ACTUAL_2$, the
correlations are 0.925 for dominance and 0.924 for anticipation. These
are extremely small differences.

Second, testing the predictions of the dominance model with direct
hypothesis tests shows slightly more support for anticipation at the
$\alpha = 0.10$ level. Overall, using $ACTUAL_1$ (see Tables 4.12 and 4.13),

Table 4.12: *BOG Hypothesis Tests 2, Data for the Hypothesis Tests*

APPT.	RANGE	PRED	$ACTUAL_1$	$ACTUAL_2$
1	1	0.899	0.899	0.966
2	1	1.430	1.585	1.499
3	1	1.585	1.585	1.506
4	1	1.430	1.585	1.342
5	1	1.585	1.650	1.632
6	1	1.650	1.650	1.639
7	1	1.650	1.650	1.629
8	1	1.650	1.650	1.524
9	3	1.409	1.505	1.524
10	3	1.409	1.505	1.522
11	1	1.505	1.582	1.537
12	1	1.582	1.582	1.523
13	3	1.295	1.295	1.203
14	3	1.295	1.295	1.203
15	3	1.219	0.469	0.624
16	3	0.448	0.448	0.486
17	3	0.448	0.448	0.469
18	3	0.469	0.469	0.551
19	1	0.469	0.617	0.598
20	1	0.617	0.777	0.904
21	1	0.777	0.857	0.915
22	1	1.535	1.535	1.349
23	1	1.535	1.535	1.349

Table 4.13: *BOG Hypothesis Tests 2, Results*

APPT.	ACTUAL$_1$					ACTUAL$_2$				
	NULL	ALTERNATIVE	z	p	ACCEPT NULL?[a]	NULL	ALTERNATIVE	z	p	ACCEPT NULL?[a]
1					yes	P <= A	P > A	0.402	0.344	yes
2	P <= A	P > A	0.511	0.305	yes	P <= A	P > A	0.470	0.319	yes
3					yes	P >= A	P < A	−0.582	0.280	yes
4	P <= A	P > A	0.511	0.305	yes	P >= A	P < A	−0.493	0.311	yes
5	P <= A	P > A	0.244	0.404	yes	P <= A	P > A	0.376	0.353	yes
6					yes	P >= A	P < A	−0.093	0.463	yes
7					yes	P >= A	P < A	−0.174	0.431	yes
8					yes	P >= A	P < A	−1.048	0.147	yes
9	P <= A	P > A	0.332	0.370	yes	P <= A	P > A	0.957	0.169	yes
10	P <= A	P > A	0.332	0.370	yes	P <= A	P > A	0.894	0.186	yes
11	P <= A	P > A	0.275	0.392	yes	P <= A	P > A	0.258	0.398	yes
12					yes	P >= A	P < A	−0.437	0.331	yes
13					yes	P >= A	P < A	−0.463	0.322	yes
14					yes	P >= A	P < A	−0.463	0.322	yes
15	P >= A	P < A	−3.388	0.000	no	P >= A	P < A	−2.928	0.002	no
16					yes	P <= A	P > A	0.248	0.402	yes
17					yes	P <= A	P > A	0.148	0.441	yes
18					yes	P <= A	P > A	0.552	0.290	yes
19	P <= A	P > A	0.470	0.319	yes	P <= A	P > A	0.840	0.200	yes
20	P <= A	P > A	0.519	0.302	yes	P <= A	P > A	1.982	0.024	no
21	P <= A	P > A	0.351	0.363	yes	P <= A	P > A	0.893	0.190	yes
22					yes	P >= A	P < A	−0.912	0.181	yes
23					yes	P >= A	P < A	−0.912	0.181	yes
					22					21

[a] At the 0.10 level

the dominance model predicts twenty-two appointments while anticipation predicts twenty-three; with $ACTUAL_2$, dominance predicts twenty-one and anticipation also predicts twenty-one.

The two models differ on six appointments: 15, 19, 20, 21, 22, and 23. First, with $ACTUAL_1$, on appointments 15, 19, 22, and 23, presidential dominance better predicts the outcome, while on the other two, the predictions are virtually identical. On the last two appointments, 22 and 23, presidential dominance exactly predicts the outcomes, while anticipation only significantly predicts them. Second, with $ACTUAL_2$, anticipation better predicts the outcome on appointments 15, 19, 20, and 21, but appointments 15 and 20 are extremely close calls. The bottom line is that both make very similar predictions with regard to the BOG, and both are generally successful in predicting the outcomes.

The regression results are also ambiguous (Table 4.14). As was the case with the FOMC, testing the *PRED* model against the *PRES* model:

$$H_0 : ACTUAL_i = \beta_0 + \beta_1 PRED_i + \epsilon_i \qquad (4.11)$$

$$H_a : ACTUAL_i = \beta_0 + \beta_1 PRES_i + \epsilon_i \qquad (4.12)$$

results in support for the *PRED* model. The Cox and J statistics are respectively -0.285 ($p = 0.388$) and -0.761 ($p = 0.223$). For the reverse hypotheses, the Cox and J statistics are respectively -39.347 and 10.008.

Table 4.14: *BOG Hypothesis Tests 2, Regression Results*

	Dependent Variable: $ACTUAL_2$		
	Coefficient	Coefficient	Coefficient
C	0.987	0.120	0.162
	(−0.09)	(−8.59)	(−8.56)
PRES	0.211		
	(−6.80)		
PRED		0.908	
		(−1.13)	
PRESPRED			0.853
			(−1.94)
Number of Observations	23	23	23
R-squared	0.129	0.855	0.856
Corrected R-squared	0.088	0.848	0.849
Sum of Squared Residuals	3.244	0.542	0.537
Standard Error of the Regression	0.393	0.161	0.160

t-statistics for $H_0 : \beta = 1$ are in parentheses; for the model to be true, it is best to accept the null

However, in the more fair test of the *PRED* versus the *PRESPRED* model:

$$H_0 : ACTUAL_i = \beta_0 + \beta_1 PRED_i + \epsilon_i \qquad (4.13)$$

$$H_a : ACTUAL_i = \beta_0 + \beta_1 PRESPRED_i + \epsilon_i \qquad (4.14)$$

the results of the forward hypothesis tests contradict the results of the reverse tests. The Cox and J statistics for the hypotheses as written – the forward tests – are respectively -2.330 and 1.854. Thus we would reject the null, the *PRED* model, in favor of the alternative model, the *PRESPRED* model. However, the Cox and J statistics for the *PRESPRED* model as the null and the *PRED* model as the alternative – the reverse tests – are respectively -2.26 and 1.80. Thus based on this set of tests, we reject the null, the *PRESPRED* model, in favor of the alternative, the *PRED* model.

Thus the results are rather inconclusive. The evidence can go either way on anticipation versus dominance with respect to the BOG. Definitive answers await further observations on appointments that will allow for the examination of greater numbers of different predictions from the two models.

4.5 POLICY EFFECTS

Up to this point, we do not really know what this analysis means for actual policy, the interest rates set by the FOMC and the BOG. I have used the FOMC or BOG median interchangeably with the term "policy" without really examining what the medians mean for the FOMC's federal funds rate and the BOG's discount rate – the actual policy of the two bodies. In this section, I examine the relationship between the medians and the interest rates and what they mean in terms of how the appointment process model predicts policy.

First, let us examine the relationship between the FOMC median and the federal funds rate – the rate over which the FOMC has most control. The FOMC median is either $ACTUAL_1$ or $ACTUAL_2$, the FOMC median after an appointee takes office. For the federal funds rate, I used the average of the real federal funds rate from an appointee's date of appointment to the next appointee's date of appointment. For example, Jackson was appointed on May 22, 1975, and Gardner, on November 15, 1975. For Jackson's appointment, I averaged the real federal funds rate from May 1975 through October 1975. The relationship is moderate with a correlation of 0.410 for $ACTUAL_1$ and 0.422 for $ACTUAL_2$. The graph in Figure 4.3 plots the three variables: the two measures of the FOMC median ($ACTUAL_1$ and $ACTUAL_2$) and the real federal funds rate (*Federal Funds Rate*).

Going back to the direct hypothesis tests, suppose we conservatively use the $\alpha = 0.15$ level and $ACTUAL_2$; then the model correctly predicts the FOMC median 78 percent (eighteen of twenty-three) of the time. If we combine this fact with the fact that the FOMC median correlates with the average real federal funds rate at 0.422, we can predict the average federal funds rate between appointments 32.9 percent of the time.

Given that this analysis only takes into account the political process for making appointments, the results are promising. This analysis does not account for anything else including the fact that the federal funds rate is determined not only by the FOMC, but also by market forces.

Second, let us look at the relationship between the BOG median and the discount rate – the rate that the BOG controls. As for the FOMC, the BOG median is either $ACTUAL_1$ or $ACTUAL_2$, the BOG median after an appointee takes office. The discount rate is the average from the date of a nomination to the date of the next nomination. The relationship is almost identical to that for the FOMC and the real federal funds rate; the correlation between the discount rate and $ACTUAL_1$ is 0.411, while the correlation with $ACTUAL_2$ is 0.488. As before, with the same conservative assumptions, we can predict the average discount rate between appointments about 38.1 percent of the time. Figure 4.4 plots the three variables.

It is surprising that the correlation between the discount rate and $SQ2$ is not much higher for the BOG compared to the FOMC. While the FOMC cannot totally control the federal funds rate, the BOG does control the discount rate. Two points can be made in this regard. First, although the FOMC does not control the federal funds rate 100 percent, it does control it very closely; the federal funds rate is its primary target.

Second, as with the FOMC and the federal funds rate, this analysis does not take into account any other political or economic factors – only those factors associated with political appointments. Both bodies may be subject to other political pressures such as direct pressures from the president or Congress, or to economic pressures such as that caused by rising oil prices. Although averaging over time smooths out some of those factors, it does not eradicate all of them. In both cases, these factors will influence the correlation. Given that this is the case, it is still encouraging that the correlations are as high as they are.

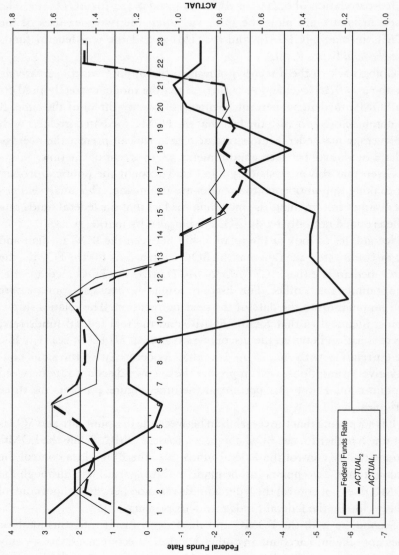

Figure 4.3: The FOMC Median and the Real Federal Funds Rate

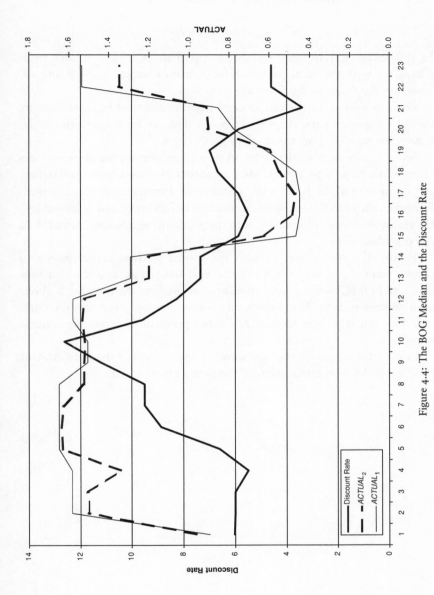

Figure 4.4: The BOG Median and the Discount Rate

4.6 SUMMARY

In this chapter, I directly tested the predictions of the model from Chapter 2 with the ideal point estimates from Chapter 3. By doing so, I answered two of the book's main questions.

First, in answer to the question of whether political influence occurs through appointments, the answer is – it does. In both institutions, the results strongly support the model's predictions.

Second, in answer to the question of who influences, the answer is less clear. With respect to the FOMC, anticipation does better on balance, but in the case of the BOG, anticipation and dominance do equally well. However, the FOMC is the more important policy body, and at least there, the results indicate influence by both the president and Senate, rather than the president alone.

Finally, the results suggest that the model predicts actual policy to some extent. In terms of both the federal funds rate and the discount rate, the FOMC median after appointment predicts the rates with about 32.9 percent success. The success rate is encouraging given that the analysis does not take into account any other political or economic context variables.

In the next chapter, I examine another application of the appointment process model – an application to the newly created ECB.

5

Appointments to the European Central Bank

Italy's membership in the EMU was unthinkable in early 1996. At that time, Italy fulfilled none of the Maastricht convergence criteria, a number of economic requirements for entry into the EMU.[38] Among European Union (EU) countries, with the exception of Greece, Italy's budget deficit, inflation rate, and interest rates were the highest, and its gross debt was the second highest. In addition, the Italian lira left the Exchange Rate Mechanism (ERM) in 1992.

Within months, the situation changed drastically. In the fall, Italy released its budget forecasts for 1997 and 1998 (*Financial Times*, September 28, 1996). Surprisingly, the deficit figures nearly achieved the 3 percent convergence criterion level, which raised expectations of Italy's entrance into EMU. Consequently, the Italian inflation and interest rates began to drop, and Italy rejoined the ERM (*Financial Times*, November 25, 1996). Combined with the fact that the German and French budgets

---

[38] The Maastricht Treaty is the Treaty on European Union signed in 1992 in the Dutch city of Maastricht. There are four main criteria based on price stability, government fiscal position, the ERM, and interest rates. The criteria are defined in Articles 104c, 109j, and the Protocols on the Excessive Deficit Procedure and the Convergence Criteria. For price stability, a member state's average inflation rate over the year before examination cannot exceed that of the three best performing states in terms of price stability. The deficit criteria are "3% for the ratio of planned or actual government deficit to gross domestic product at market prices," and "60% for the ratio of government debt to gross domestic product at market prices" (Art. 1, Protocol on the Excessive Deficit Procedure). For the ERM, the currency of a country must have stayed for at least two years within the normal bands of fluctuations "without severe tensions" and without devaluations (Art. 3, Protocol on the Convergence Criteria). Finally, for the interest rate, a country's average nominal long-term interest rate (usually the ten-year government bond rate) cannot exceed by more than two percentage points that of the three best countries in terms of price stability (Art. 4, Protocol on the Convergence Criteria).

indicated problems with the 3 percent level and that the Belgian gross debt was even higher than the Italian debt, Italy's prospects looked markedly better.

Still, the core EMU countries[39] forcefully raised concerns about Italy's economic fitness for EMU entry. French president Jacques Chirac stated that Italy needed to get its financial house in order and that, "[joining EMU] may take a little bit longer for those who are further behind, like Italy" (*Financial Times*, October 2, 1996). Hans Tietmeyer, president of the German Bundesbank, proclaimed, "Italy certainly has more to do" (*Financial Times*, November 29, 1996). The concerns culminated in a possible plan for Italy's late entry into EMU, which Italy angrily rejected (*Financial Times*, February 7, 1997). Despite the considerable hoopla, in the end, Italy was a founding member of the then eleven-country EMU in 1998.[40]

What was the basis of the concerns regarding Italy? It is not clear. In the press and in academic circles, the concerns themselves centered on the past economic and political instability of Italy and its potential future contribution to easy monetary policy and a weak euro (Coleman 1998; Kosters, et. al. 1998). But what was the exact path from Italy's EMU membership to easy policy and a weak euro? It is as if the naysayers envisioned a sort of mean monetary policy among the preferred policies of the member countries: because Italy's preferred policy was historically very easy and its currency very weak, Italy's entry would automatically lead to easier policy by dragging down the mean.

As this chapter shows, these arguments neglect the political institutions of European monetary policy – the new ECB, the appointment process by which the ECB's members are appointed, and how that process influences policy. This chapter demonstrates that a mean monetary policy is never the case, and Italian influence can be very limited.

The impact of a single country is generally limited; it cannot unduly influence the ECB. The reason: the EMU founders created a highly independent ECB, which when combined with the appointment process and the conditions at the start of EMU, guaranteed tight policy for years to come. First, the founders created an appointment process that locked in the current policy at the start of EMU. Second, the current policy at EMU's start was relatively tight due to expansionary economic growth

---

[39] Austria, Belgium, France, Germany, Luxembourg, and the Netherlands.
[40] The other ten members were Austria, Belgium, France, Luxembourg, Germany, the Netherlands, Ireland, Finland, Spain, and Portugal. Greece joined in January 2001.

at the time. Third, the founders shielded the ECB from political influence by providing an explicit price stability mandate, lacking even of the Bundesbank and the Fed, and severely minimizing the ECB's responsibility to other governmental institutions.

Along this line of reasoning, this chapter examines the ECB's appointment process and attempts to answer three sets of questions – two of which correspond to those for the Fed. First, what is the appointment process? Second, who influences appointments? Third, what does the process mean for the direction of monetary policy?

To answer the first two questions, I adapt the appointment process model from Chapter 2 to the ECB appointment process. In the process, the veto power of each Head of State drives two sets of results. In the first, the model demonstrates that extreme Heads of States, those who prefer the most easy or most tight policy, can dominate the process by virtue of their veto power. Second, the model shows that the Heads of States can easily deadlock and agree only to disagree; they maintain the current status quo.

As for the third question, under a reasonable set of assumptions regarding the situation at the time of the initial appointments, the chapter predicts that the appointments made in May of 1998 will preserve the pre-May status quo policy – relatively tight, low-inflation monetary policy. This result counters the alarm regarding the entry of the noncore countries, that is Italy as well as Spain, Portugal, and Greece.[41]

The model in this chapter also shows how single countries like Italy can be limited in their influence on the ECB. The model further provides a framework for considering the implications of EMU's enlargement. Greece's recent membership loosened policy slightly, partially in line with the model's prediction. The chapter also briefly considers the potential memberships of Sweden, the United Kingdom, and the ten new members of the EU in 2004.

5.1 A COMPARISON OF THE UNITED STATES AND EUROPEAN MONETARY UNION MONETARY SYSTEMS

The European System of Central Banks (ESCB), which began functioning on January 1, 1999, has many similarities to the Federal Reserve System. Despite the similarities, key institutional differences emphasize the most

---

[41] The entrance of Ireland and Finland never raised the level of concern directed at the three southern countries.

obvious difference between the two monetary systems – that the U.S. system functions within a single unified federal government whereas the European system does not. As a result, the European system emphasizes federal (national) rather than central (EU) power to set monetary policy, whereas the opposite is true in the Federal Reserve System.

5.1.1 The Appointing Actors

Nowhere is this difference more apparent than in the actors involved in the appointment process, and more specifically, the powers of those actors. Three sets of EU actors are statutorily involved in the appointment process. First, the *European Councils* are summits of the Heads of States of the fifteen EU member countries[42] in which decisions are made by common accord, that is unanimity rule. Second, the *Council of Ministers* consists of the cabinet ministers from the fifteen EU countries. Depending on the type of issue, the council makes decisions by unanimity rule or qualified majority (a 71 percent majority; see Table 5.1)[43] in which larger countries vote with more weight.[44] Third, the *European Parliament* is the EU's popularly elected legislature. The European Parliament makes decisions by simple majority; the larger countries have more European Parliament representatives.

All truly important EU decisions – for example, EMU's creation, its membership, and central bank appointees – have been made in the European Councils at the level of the Heads of States. In the United States, this would be comparable to having the state governors decide crucial national issues by a unanimous vote. Lesser decisions are made by the Council of Ministers and the European Parliament, which together have the power to pass EU laws and the budget. But between the two, the European Parliament is much less powerful. For example, on taxation, the European Parliament can only provide nonbinding opinions.

This general pattern holds true for the ECB's appointment process. Regarding the process, the Maastricht Treaty, Article 11.2 of the Statute

---

[42] Austria, Belgium, Denmark, Finland, France, Germany, Greece, Ireland, Italy, Luxembourg, the Netherlands, Portugal, Spain, Sweden, and the United Kingdom.

[43] A qualified majority is sixty-two votes of the eighty-seven possible votes in the Council of Ministers (71 percent).

[44] Particular sets of ministers decide on the issues for which they are responsible in their home countries; finance ministers decide on issues relating to monetary policy.

Table 5.1: *Voting Weights in the European Union*

	European Parliament		Council of Ministers	
	Votes	% of Total Votes	Votes	% of Total Votes
Germany	99	15.81%	10	11.49%
France	87	13.90%	10	11.49%
Italy	87	13.90%	10	11.49%
United Kingdom	87	13.90%	10	11.49%
Spain	64	10.22%	8	9.20%
Netherlands	31	4.95%	5	5.75%
Belgium	25	3.99%	5	5.75%
Greece	25	3.99%	5	5.75%
Portugal	25	3.99%	5	5.75%
Sweden	22	3.51%	4	4.60%
Austria	21	3.35%	4	4.60%
Denmark	16	2.56%	3	3.45%
Finland	16	2.56%	3	3.45%
Ireland	15	2.40%	3	3.45%
Luxembourg	6	0.96%	2	12.30%
TOTAL	626		87	

Source: European Union

of the ESCB states:

"...the President, the Vice President, and other members of the Executive Board shall be appointed from among persons of recognized standing and professional experience in monetary or banking matters by common accord of the government of the Member States at the level of the Heads of State or Government, on a recommendation from the Council after it has consulted the European Parliament and the Governing Council."

The treaty's language implies the following sequence for the appointment process. First, the European Parliament and the Governing Council, the main decision-making body of the ECB, suggest potential nominees. Second, the Council of Ministers recommends the suggested nominees or makes its own recommendation. Third, the Heads of States can approve the recommendation or choose someone else altogether.

However, neither recommendations nor consultations are binding. Thus in reality, the Heads of States hold all the cards; neither the European Parliament nor the Governing Council has any real power in this process. In its recommendation role, the Council of Ministers ultimately seems powerless as well, especially since the ministers are all cabinet members in their home countries, handpicked by the respective Heads of States.

This unequal distribution of power was apparent at the May 1998 European Council, when the first appointees were chosen. Except for a row over the ECB presidency, the appointment choices were a *fait accompli* with clear prior agreement among the Heads of States. Over the previous few months, finance ministers and central bankers influenced the choices, but seemingly through their own heads of states rather than through the various EU institutions. The subsequent European Parliament reviews of the appointees were largely uneventful and resulted in the unsurprisingly high majority recommendations of the candidates.

A similar process occurred when a new appointment opportunity arose in 2002 – the first since the start of EMU. This time, the Heads of States, through the Council of Ministers, chose Greece's Lucas Papademos to replace Christian Noyer as the new vice president. A slight problem occurred when the Belgians abstained due to their preference for their own candidate, Paul de Grauwe, but the Belgians later agreed to Papademos. In the weeks following, the European Parliament, Governing Council, and European Council essentially rubber stamped the choice.

The distribution of powers in this process differs substantially from that in the Fed appointment process. In the latter, a major difference is that both sets of actors, the president and Senate, are from central government institutions. Furthermore, although the Senate represents state interests, in the appointment process, both the president and Senate have different binding powers that constrain one another. The president has proposal power, but his proposal must be approved by the Senate. The Senate cannot bypass the president with proposals of its own. The difference in the ECB process is that the Council of Ministers' proposals, unlike the president's proposals, are not binding. If the Heads of States decide against the proposals, they can propose and appoint their own candidates. The Senate, on the other hand, must await a favorable presidential nominee. Thus in the ECB process, the preferences of the Heads of States are ultimately supreme – it is all about the federal units – whereas in the Fed process, both the president and Senate's preferences matter – the central units matter as well.

5.1.2 *The Institutions of Monetary Policy*

In terms of who appoints, the individual countries maintain control versus the EU institutions. Furthermore, even if all the Heads of States agree on the appointees, these centrally appointed members do not alone control monetary policy. The structure of the monetary institutions limits their powers. This again contrasts with the Federal Reserve System in which, once appointed, the central appointees have majority power.

At first glance, the two sets of institutions look very similar. First, both systems are federal. The Federal Reserve System consists of twelve district reserve banks, one for each region of the country. The ESCB consists of twelve national central banks, one for each EMU country.

However, an important difference lies in the boundaries of the federal units. On the ESCB, national borders determine those boundaries. For the Federal Reserve System, the district lines bound regional areas with economic centers *from the year 1913*; the boundaries have remained fixed since then. Thus the ESCB's boundaries are of countries with defined national interests and political power at the EU level. Nothing could be farther from the truth for the Fed, whose district boundaries cross state lines and define, in some cases, obsolete centers of former financial prowess.

Second, two central decision-making institutions control both federal systems, but the balance of power between the central and federal units is reversed in each system.[45] Similar to the Fed's central structure, the ESCB has two central decision-making bodies: the Executive Board and the Governing Council, which are comparable to the BOG and the FOMC respectively (see Table 5.2).[46] These two institutions make up the ECB.

The Executive Board. The Executive Board consists of six members: a president, vice president, and four other members (Art. 11.1, Statute of the ESCB). The president and vice president are also the Governing Council's president and vice president. The Executive Board members must be citizens of the member states and are appointed to staggered, eight-year, nonrenewable terms by the Heads of States on recommendation from the Council of Ministers who consult with the European Parliament and the Governing Council of the ECB (Art. 11.2, Statute of the ESCB).

The Executive Board is responsible for the implementation of monetary policy and the preparation of the Governing Council's meetings (Art. 12.1, 12.2, Statute of the ESCB). It makes decisions using a simple majority rule

[45] Both sets of regional banks have no decision-making powers with respect to monetary policy. The main function of the ESCB's national banks is to act as depositories of reserves, and the Fed's reserve banks clear checks for the payments system and regulates banks in the regions.
[46] The Protocol on the Statute of the European System of Central Banks and of the European Central Banks sets out the structure and functions of the ESCB and ECB. Henceforth, I will refer to this protocol as the Statute of the ESCB.

Table 5.2: *The Structure of the European System of Central Banks*

Institution	Number of Members	Functions
Executive Board	6–President, Vice President, 4 other members	Implementation of monetary policy
Governing Council	6+ number of EMU countries: The first 6 are executive board members with the remaining members each representing one EMU member	Formulation of monetary policy
National Central Banks	One bank for each member state	Mainly depositories of reserves

with the President casting the decisive vote in the case of a tie (Art. 11.5, Statute of the ESCB). Just as all BOG members are also members of the FOMC in the Federal Reserve System, all Executive Board members are also members of the Governing Council, which is the main monetary policy decision-making body.

The Governing Council. The Governing Council consists of the Executive Board members and the national bank governors. EMU started with eleven members with Greece rounding it out to twelve in 2001. Thus the Governing Council has eighteen members: the six Executive Board members plus one governor from each of the twelve national banks.

The appointment procedures for the national bank governors may vary, but the Maastricht Treaty and the Statute of the ESCB mandate certain basic requirements. First, once appointed, national bank governors cannot take instructions from their governments or EU institutions (Art. 107, Title II of the Maastricht Treaty; Art. 7, Statute of the ESCB). Second, the terms of each governors' office must last at least five years (Art. 14.2, Statute of the ESCB). Third, appointees cannot be dismissed unless "he no longer fulfills the conditions required for the performance of his duties or if he has been guilty of serious misconduct" (Art. 14.2, Statute of the ESCB).

The primary function of the Governing Council is to formulate monetary policy (Art. 12.1, Statute of the ESCB). The treaty specifies that this function may include the setting of intermediate monetary objectives, key interest rates, and the supply of reserves in the ESCB (Art. 12.1, Statute of

98

the ESCB). The Governing Council makes decisions on the basis of simple majority rule with the president casting the decisive vote in the case of a tie.

A key difference between the FOMC and the Governing Council – the main decision-making bodies for monetary policy in each system – is the balance of power between the central government and the federal units. On the FOMC, presidential appointees, the BOG members, control the majority; of the twelve members, the regional reserve bank presidents occupy only five of the twelve seats. On the Governing Council, the EU appointees, the Executive Board members, are a minority; the national central bank governors make up twelve of the eighteen members. As in the ECB appointment process, the federal elements are emphasized over the central elements. The structure of the ECB's Governing Board ensures that national interests are represented over pan-European interests.

In theory, the ECB is the most independent central bank in the world. The statutes do not specify its responsibility to anyone; the ECB does not have to defend its actions to any EU or national body, although it does have to provide annual reports to the European Commission, European Parliament, Council of Ministers, and European Council (Art. 15, Statute of the ESCB). Even the Fed, considered one of the most independent central banks in the world, until recently had to defend its actions to the U.S. Congress in semiannual monetary policy hearings. Furthermore, the Fed is ultimately responsible to Congress (which can alter the basic Fed law with the President's signature). Changing the ESCB statutes requires unanimity of the European Council and possibly referenda in the various EU countries.

The irony is that despite its independence, it can be highly immobile in policy due to its structure. As the subsequent sections show, unanimous approval of nominees makes it very difficult to move long-term policy. Furthermore, even if the appointees would like to move policy, national bank governors can stop policy movement by ganging up against the appointees. Both of these features, especially the appointment process, have the potential to render the ECB the most immobile of central banks, even if it is the most independent.

5.2 THE MODEL

5.2.1 The Model's Assumptions

1. *Actors and their preferences.* The actors are the Heads of States (HS) and the Governing Council (GC) of the ECB. The assumptions about

preferences are essentially identical to those previously stated: all individuals have well-behaved preferences defined on a single dimension of monetary policy measured by the short-term real interest rate $r \in [0, 1]$ on a scale of lower to higher rates representing respectively easier to tighter policy. A utility function for an individual i is, as before, in the form, $U_i = \theta(|r_i - SQ|)$ in which r_i is the individual's ideal real interest rate, SQ is the current real interest rate implied by the median member of the Governing Council, and θ is a monotone, decreasing function. As in the Fed model, particular appointments do not enter the utility functions, and individuals care about the effects of appointments on policy rather than about the appointments themselves.

2. *Actions.* The Heads of States can unanimously choose a nominee, x, on the set of $r \in [0, 1]$; the nominee maps to a specific GC median, $SQ2$. The next section describes the exact mapping. The Governing Council members vote on monetary policy according to the rule: Vote = tighter policy if $r_i > SQ$, Vote = easier policy otherwise.

3. *Other assumptions and implications.* As in the Fed model, complete and perfect information characterizes this game. I also assume, as before, that the Heads of States are perfectly informed about the locations of the national bank governors. Like the FOMC, the Governing Council is a majority rule institution, and from the preceding assumptions, the median voter theorem applies. As for the Heads of States, I assume unanimity rule because they must unanimously approve the appointees.

4. *Definition: appointments and policy.* Policy in this model refers specifically to the Governing Council's formulation of monetary policy. For appointments, however, the focus is on the Executive Board appointments. But I am only interested in these appointments insofar as they affect the Governing Council's policy, much as I previously concentrated on the BOG appointments as they affected FOMC policy.

An alternative is to focus explicitly on the Executive Board's policy because it does have potentially important policy-implementation powers. However, it is not yet clear whether these powers will be consequential; to date, most of the action seems to have been on the Governing Council. If history is any guide, in the Federal Reserve System, the Federal Reserve Bank of New York has powers similar to those of the Executive Board, but under the institutional reforms of 1935, the New York Fed has very little discretion. In fact, the Maastricht Treaty's language does not grant the Executive Board much power independent of the Governing Council:

"The Executive Board shall implement monetary policy *in accordance with the guidelines and decisions laid down by the Governing Council....* In addition the Executive Board may have certain powers delegated to it *where the Governing Council so decides*" (Art. 12.1, Statute of the ESCB, emphasis added).

An important question regards how the Executive Board appointments translate to the monetary policy set by the Governing Council. The Executive Board members are the only ones on the Governing Council appointed by EU-level institutions. All other members are national bank governors, who are appointed by a myriad of different institutions and procedures in different countries. The national bank governors outnumber the Executive Board members twelve to six. The opposite is true on the Fed in which presidential appointees outnumber the reserve bank presidents seven to five.

Nevertheless, despite their relative small numbers, the Executive Board could have substantial influence on monetary policy depending on how they match up to the national bank governors in terms of policy preferences. If the Executive Board members are all on one side of the policy dimension, for example, then their influence will tend to be smaller than if they are dispersed among the other Governing Council members. In the latter situation, it is more likely that one of the Executive Board members will be the median, policy-determining member. Dispersion rather than the extremity of Executive Board members is somewhat more likely as all heads of the member states, who may all have different policy preferences, must approve the Executive Board appointees.

5.2.2 Sequence

This game is much more simple compared to the Fed game. For each appointment opportunity, each Head of State simultaneously proposes a point as the new policy point, $SQ2$. The proposal that garners unanimous support is the RR equilibrium policy. Depending on the range of possible outcomes, the Heads of States make an appointment that achieves either the RR equilibrium policy or the closest boundary point, L or H.

5.2.3 Possible Outcomes

As mentioned previously, Greece joined EMU in 2001. Thus there are now twelve EMU countries and an eighteen-member Governing Council.

But to assess the implications of the important 1998 appointment process in Section 5.3, the following exposition of the model sticks with the initial setup in 1998 with eleven Heads of States and a seventeen-member Governing Council. The results follow for an eighteen-member Governing Council with slight adjustments of seat numbers and medians.

The possible outcomes are analogous to those for the BOG that, like the 1998 seventeen-member Governing Council, has an odd rather than even number of members. There are three ranges defined by (1) the first eight seats, (2) the ninth median seat, and (3) the last eight seats. As with the FOMC members, the Governing Council members are numbered in order of easiest to tightest policy, $x1$ to $x17$.

Range 1: *if* $y \in \{x1, x2, \ldots, x8\}$

For any $y \in \{x1, x2, \ldots, x8\}$, $SQ1 = \frac{x9+x10}{2}$. The nonunique correspondences between x and $SQ2$ are defined for any x such that:

$$(1)\ x \leq x9 \quad \Rightarrow \quad SQ2 = x9 = SQ0 = L1$$
$$(2)\ x \geq x10 \quad \Rightarrow \quad SQ2 = x10 = H1$$

The unique correspondences are defined for any x such that:

$$(3)\ x9 < x < x10 \quad \Rightarrow \quad L1 < SQ2 = x < H1$$

Range 2: *if* $y \in \{x9\}$

For any $y \in \{x9\}$, $SQ1 = \frac{x8+x10}{2}$. The nonunique correspondences are:

$$(1)\ x \leq x8 \quad \Rightarrow \quad SQ2 = x8 = L2 < L1$$
$$(2)\ x \geq x10 \quad \Rightarrow \quad SQ2 = x10 = H2 = H1$$

The unique correspondences are:

$$(3)\ x8 < x < x10 \quad \Rightarrow \quad L2 < SQ2 = x < H2$$

Range 3: *if* $y \in \{x10, x11, \ldots, x17\}$

For any $y \in \{x10, x11, \ldots, x17\}$, $SQ1 = \frac{x8+x9}{2}$. The nonunique correspondences are:

$$(1)\ x \leq x8 \quad \Rightarrow \quad SQ2 = x8 = L3 = L2 < L1$$
$$(2)\ x \geq x9 \quad \Rightarrow \quad SQ2 = x9 = H3 < H1 = H2$$

The unique correspondences are:

$$(3)\ x8 < x < x10 \quad \Rightarrow \quad L3 < SQ2 = x < H3$$

In overall comparisons, Range 2 is the largest of all three. Whether Range 1 is greater than Range 3 and vice versa depends on the distance between $x9$ and $x10$ for Range 1 and between $x8$ and $x9$ for Range 3.

5.2.4 *Actual Outcomes: Adding the Heads of States*

In the Fed game, the president and Senate first agree on a RR equilibrium policy. Given the range of possible outcomes, depending on the location of the retiree, the president and Senate then try to get as close as possible to the RR equilibrium policy.

The setup is quite similar with respect to the ECB game with two key differences. First, there is no agenda setter. There is no one akin to the president in this game. Second, there is a unanimity requirement; each Head of State must unanimously approve any policy point. If we were to apply both these features analogously to the Fed game, there would be no president, and it would be as if each senator, rather than the Senate median, makes a proposal, and each senator must approve a proposal in order for it to pass.

The exact location of the actual policy ($SQ2$) depends on (1) the location of the Heads of States relative to the current policy ($SQ1$), and (2) the location of the existing Governing Council members. Based on (1), there are two cases. In Case 1: dominance by extreme heads of states, all of the Heads of States are on one side of the status quo. In these situations, the most extreme heads of states dictate exactly how far policy will go.

In Case 2: deadlock, at least one Head of State is on the opposite side of the status quo from the others. In this case, there is deadlock, and policy will not move because any proposed move will be vetoed by at least one Head of State. For example, suppose all Heads of States are to the left of the status quo, and the Netherlands is to the right of the status quo. Then the Netherlands rejects all movements to the left of the status quo, and the others reject all movements to the right of the status quo.

Case 1: Dominance by Extreme Heads of States

Head of State Indifference Point. Similar to the definition for the Senate indifference point, define a Head of State's indifference point as HS^-, where $|HS - SQ1| = |HS - HS^-|$.

Heads of States Labels. The Heads of States are numbered consecutively from left to right in order of easiest to tightest policy and labeled $HS1$ through $HS11$.

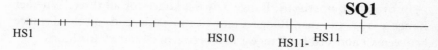

Figure 5.1: Example 1, Case 1

Figure 5.2: Example 2, Case 1

In this case, all of the Heads of States are either on the left or right side of $SQ1$. Within Case 1, there are two possible types of situations with two possible sets of outcomes.

First, suppose that there does not exist any other Head of State in the range between the most extreme Head of State (either $HS1$ or $HS11$) and her indifference point ($HS1^-$ or $HS11^-$). If they are all on the left side of $SQ1$, any one of them can propose the indifference point for the right-most Head of State, the eleventh member, $HS11^-$ (see Figure 5.1). This point will be closer to the ideal points of every other Head of State, and thus, the Heads of States will collectively approve this point as the new policy point. Analogously, if the Heads of States are all on the right side of $SQ1$, a Head of State can propose the indifference point of the first member, $HS1^-$, and it will be unanimously approved as the new policy point. The Heads of States will then make the appointment to get as close as possible to that new policy point.

More formally,

(1) if $HS \leq SQ1$ *and* $\forall HS, \;\; HS \leq HS11^-$
$$\Rightarrow SQ2 = HS11^- \text{ if } HS11^- \in [L, H], \; SQ2 = L \text{ } otherwise$$
(2) if $HS \geq SQ1$ *and* $\forall HS, \;\; HS \geq HS1^-$
$$\Rightarrow SQ2 = HS1^- \text{ if } HS1^- \in [L, H], \; SQ2 = H \text{ } otherwise$$

Second, suppose that there does exist another Head of State (either $HS2$ or $HS10$) in the range between the most extreme Head of State and her indifference point (see Figure 5.2). Then that Head of State can propose her ideal point as the new policy point. $HS1$ through $HS9$ will agree because for each one of them, that point is closer to them than the reversion point, SQ_1. For $HS11$, $HS10$ is also in its preferred set. More formally,

(3) if $HS \leq SQ1$ *and* $HS10 \in [HS11^-, HS11]$
$\Rightarrow SQ2 = HS10$ *if* $HS10 \in [L, H]$, $SQ2 = L$ *otherwise*
(4) if $HS \geq SQ1$ *and* $HS2 \in [HS1, HS1^-]$
$\Rightarrow SQ2 = HS2^-$ *if* $HS2 \in [L, H]$, $SQ2 = H$ *otherwise*

Case 2: Deadlock. In this case, at least one Head of State is on the opposite side of $SQ1$ from at least one other Head of State. In such a case, it is impossible to move policy. Any moves to the right of SQ_1, no matter how small, will be vetoed by the Heads of States to the left of $SQ1$. Analogously, any moves to the left of $SQ1$ will be vetoed by the Heads of States to the right of $SQ1$. Thus the predicted new policy point is the same as the old policy point, $SQ1$. More formally,

(1) if there exists at least one $HS \leq SQ1$ and one $HS \geq SQ1$
$\Rightarrow SQ2 = SQ1$

What is interesting is that policy can change at all with ECB appointments. Because all Heads of States have veto power, at least one Head of State should reject any incremental policy change. That occurs in Case 2 but not in Case 1. The model shows that when all the Heads of States agree on the direction of change, all gain from some policy movement. But all such movements are potentially small since they are dictated by the most extreme Head of State.

What influence does a traditionally inflationary country like Italy have? With its one national bank seat, Italy automatically does move policy a bit in an easier direction. In terms of influence on the appointment process, it depends on the case. In Case 1, a country like Italy can potentially have much positive policy influence, positive in the sense of moving policy. Italy could in fact dictate the outcome. But if the extreme country is not Italy, then Italy has absolutely no influence, and the fears are unjustified. In Case 2, Italy can only have a negative effect on policy; it can only dictate that policy will not change at all. While Italy also has this power in Case 1, it will not be in Italy's interest to veto policy moves because the new policy makes it better off.

Thus there is always some reason for concern in adding the membership of an inflationary country because that country does get a minimum of one seat on the Governing Council and that moves policy in an easier direction. But the extent of further influence is rather limited due to the setup of the appointment process. Basically the model delineates when a particular country is influential and when it is not. The question is, what situation characterized the initial situation in May of 1998, when the Heads of States made the first ECB appointments? Section 5.3 tries to answer this question.

5.2.5 *Extensions and Comparisons to the Fed*

In the ECB game, the veto power of each Head of State and the lack of an agenda setter drives the major differences in policy outcomes compared to the Fed game.

First, veto power means that extreme regional interests can influence ECB policy to a much greater extent than Fed policy. The only way to move policy in the ECB setup is to satisfy, in Case 1, the most extreme or the two most extreme Heads of States. Without the support of either $HS1$ or $HS11$, the policy reverts back to the status quo.

On the Fed, the analogous setup would be if all the Senate members had the right to veto the president's choice; then the senators closest to the status quo would have the most influence. But with majority rule in the Senate, the influence of extreme interests is very limited because the president only has to satisfy the moderate, by definition, Senate median; forty-nine senators can disagree with the president, but as long as he obtains fifty-one votes, policy will move to his proposed point.

Second, veto power also means that the ECB appointment process favors the status quo policy while the Fed's process does not. Disagreement is guaranteed in all "Case 2: deadlock" situations, when at least one Head of State is on the opposite side of $SQ1$ from the other Heads of States. Whereas one veto is enough for deadlock to occur in the ECB game, deadlock is less likely in the Fed game because it requires fifty-one senators to be on the other side of the status quo from the president.

Third, the addition of agenda-setting powers only changes the outcomes slightly, if at all, in the ECB game, while they can dramatically change the outcomes of the Fed game. For the ECB, the extent of possible change depends on who is designated the agenda setter. On the one hand, if the agenda setter was the Council of Ministers, a non–Head of State, the outcomes would not change over those of the current setup. Consider the case when all Heads of States are left of $SQ1$. In this Case 1 situation, the Council of Ministers would have to choose either $HS11^-$ or $HS10$ – the outcomes without the agenda setter. On the other hand, if

$HS11$ were the agenda setter, the outcome would be $HS11$'s ideal point – different from the previous outcomes of $HS11^-$ or $HS10$.

Still, in a comparison of the sheer magnitude of policy changes, the Council of Ministers as agenda setter would lead to bigger changes than the Heads of States as agenda setters. Both $HS11^-$ and $HS10$, the outcomes with the Council of Ministers as the agenda setter, are farther from the status quo than $HS11$ – the outcome with $HS11$ as the agenda setter.

If an agenda setter were to be chosen, the Council of Ministers seems the more likely choice than $HS11$. It is difficult to believe that the appointment process would ever change to accommodate the most extreme Head of State because all other Heads of States must approve this change. It is easier to envision the delegation of binding proposal power to the Council of Ministers by a qualified majority, since the EU Heads of States have made greater numbers of important decisions in this fashion.

But even with the Council of Ministers as the agenda setter, the changes are potentially very small. In contrast, the outcomes in the Fed game would be quite different if, for instance, the Senate set the agenda rather than the president. In Case 2 of the current Fed game, when the president is farther from the status quo compared to the Senate, the president sometimes gets his ideal point as the outcome – he sometimes still dominates. If, however, the Senate were the agenda setter, it would sometimes dominate instead. Basically flipping the agenda setter means that the player with the agenda-setting power has much more power, whereas in the ECB game, changing the agenda setter means moving policy by a Head-of-State position or two.

In order for the possibility of greater policy change, not only would there have to be a designated agenda setter, but also a change in the unanimity rule. In the Fed setup, the agenda-setting power of the president combined with the Senate's majority rule allows for greater changes in policy. The analogous ECB setup would be if the Council of Ministers gained binding proposal power, and the Heads of States decided to accept proposals by majority rule. Then in a situation with the Council of Ministers to the left of the Heads of States and all Heads of States to the left of the status quo, the Council of Ministers would only have to propose the indifference point for $HS6$, which must be farther from $SQ1$ than either $HS10$ or $HS11^-$. But all this would only matter if the Council of Ministers could be independent from the Heads of States, and it is not clear if this could ever be the case.

Why might EMU members desire the possibility of greater policy change? There are two related reasons. First, the ECB could be more responsive to the current economic and political context without totally losing its independence. Second, with greater responsiveness, the ECB might gain more public support which is crucial for its long-term survival.

5.3 A PREDICTION

What does the preceding model mean empirically for the future monetary policy in Europe? With some reasonable assumptions about the current relevant players, I use the preceding model to predict the policy outcomes of the initial appointment process in May 1998. The prediction contradicts the recent charge that a larger monetary union with traditionally high inflation countries like Italy will necessarily mean easy monetary policy. In fact, the model shows how the institutional structure of the appointment process, together with the monetary policy status quo, ensures relatively tight monetary policy in Europe during the first four years of EMU.

The preceding model deals with the appointment process beyond the initial stages of EMU. In May of 1998, the appointment game was different; the Heads of States did not have to contend with just one Executive Board appointment but all six. Assuming that the beginning status quo was the median of the eleven-member Governing Council, the six appointments allowed the Heads of States to move the median policy point anywhere they wished; the possible outcome ranges of Section 5.2.3 did not apply.

It was a rare, one-time opportunity to move policy a great deal – if Case 1 had prevailed; recall that in Case 1, either all $HS < SQ1$ or all $HS > SQ1$, and because all the Heads of States agree on the direction of policy change, it is the only case that allows for policy change. However, as will be shown, Case 2: deadlock prevailed, and policy did not change at all.

For the first round of appointments in May 1998, a few qualifications to the appointment process were in effect. First, the Council of the European Monetary Institute (EMI), the ECB's forerunner, served in the consultation role of the Governing Council of ECB because the latter did not yet exist.[47] Second, in order to stagger the appointment terms from the

---

[47] The EMI was the forerunner of the ECB. The Council of the EMI consisted of a president and one governor from each of the fifteen national central banks (Art. 9.3, Statute of the European Monetary Institute). The Statute of the EMI is also contained in the Treaty on European Union Protocols. The Council of the EMI made decisions using a simple majority rule.

start, the president was appointed for a full term of eight years,[48] the vice president for four years, and the other four members for between five and eight years (Art. 50, Statute of the ESCB).[49] Third, non-EMU participants could not participate in the Council of Ministers' and European Council's decisions on appointees (Art. 109k, ¶3, Title II of the Maastricht Treaty).[50] Since May 1998, these nonparticipants are called "Member States with a derogation" (Art. 109k, ¶1, Title II of the Maastricht Treaty). However, the treaty does not seem to have barred such states from participating in the consultation roles provided by the European Parliament and the Council of the EMI. In reality, these countries – the United Kingdom, Sweden, and Denmark – participate in the Council of Ministers' and European Council's decisions, but the opinions that really matter are those of the EMU countries.

5.3.1 Ideal Points

Unlike the Fed, there are no voting records for the ECB. One of the first actions taken by Duisenberg was to close the records to the public for at least sixteen years. Without voting records, it is not possible to estimate ideal points for the Governing Council according to the method from Chapter 3. Similarly, it is difficult to estimate ideal points for the Heads of States.

Faced with these limitations, I used the averages of past inflation rates as a proxy for the monetary policy preferences of the various countries. From the five- and ten-year average inflation rates in Table 5.3, I constructed the following ideal points. First, for the Heads of States, I assumed that the ten-year average inflation rates of each country represent

---

[48] Although Wim Duisenberg "voluntarily" agreed to step down after four years as part of an alleged agreement between Germany and France. He recently announced his date of departure as July 2003.

[49] Therefore, the first appointment opportunity arose in 2002, followed by two in 2003, and one appointment opportunity will arise in every one of the subsequent four years. However, one of the two 2003 appointments is the president's position that is already designated to be filled by Jean-Claude Trichet, if he survives various legal inquiries. There will be no appointments in the next subsequent three years: 2007, 2008, and 2009. In 2010, the same cycle of appointments will begin again. This means that an unusually high number of appointment opportunities will arise in the first seven years of EMU.

[50] Title II of the Maastricht Treaty: Provisions Amending the Treaty Establishing the European Economic Community with a View to Establishing the European Community. Henceforth, references will be to Title II of the Maastricht Treaty.

Table 5.3: *Inflation Rates for European Union Countries*

10 years (1987–96)		5 years (1992–6)	
Netherlands	1.93	Finland	1.55
Luxembourg	2.34	Denmark	1.91
Belgium	2.36	France	1.98
Germany	2.41	Ireland	2.21
France	2.61	Belgium	2.23
Austria	2.72	Luxembourg	2.36
Denmark	2.79	Sweden	2.43
Ireland	2.69	Netherlands	2.52
Finland	3.33	Germany	2.68
United Kingdom	4.58	United Kingdom	2.73
Sweden	4.84	Austria	2.94
Italy	5.14	Italy	4.53
Spain	5.30	Spain	4.69
Portugal	8.42	Portugal	5.56
Greece	14.19	Greece	11.69

Source: IMF International Financial Statistics Line 64: Consumer Prices

the preferences of each Head of State. The ten-year period includes the period prior to 1992 when central bank independence from governments was not required. Thus this ten-year average reflects a mixture of central bankers' and governments' preferences. Inflation rates averaged over fifteen years yield an almost identical rank ordering of countries.

Second, for the members of the EMI Council, I used five-year inflation rates. In particular, for the initial $SQ1$, I used the five-year average inflation rate of the Netherlands (2.52 percent), the median of the EMI Council (see Table 5.3). After the signing of the Maastricht Treaty in 1992, countries wishing to qualify for EMU were required to grant independence to their central banks. Thus the five-year average inflation rates reflect, to a large extent, the preferences of independent central bankers. Although nonindependent central banks became independent at different times during the five-year period 1992–6, these rates are the best reflection of the central bankers' preferences.

5.3.2 May 1998: The Game, Equilibrium, and Policy Outcome

Given these assumptions, the numbers in Table 5.3 lead to the spatial configuration in Figure 5.3.

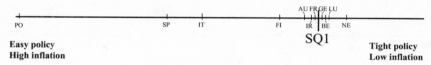

Figure 5.3: The ECB Game in May 1998

$SQ1$ is the median of the EMI Council (2.52 percent – the Netherlands), and the country acronyms stand for the Heads of States positions.[51] Because monetary policy preferences throughout this chapter are measured by the short-term interest rate, and preferences over inflation are negatively related to preferences for short-term interest rates, the figure presents the players in reverse order of inflation preferences. Thus Portugal, with the highest inflation rate, is at the lowest end of the scale in terms of short-term interest rates.

This particular configuration is a Case 2: deadlock situation, and therefore, the status quo is the equilibrium point of the game. There are seven Heads of States to the left and four to the right of the status quo.

In order to maintain $SQ1$, the equilibrium policy point, the politicians could have appointed three members of the Executive Board to the right and three members to the left of the status quo point. Alternatively, they could have appointed all six member right on the status quo point. A final option was to appoint a combination of some members on the status quo and some on either side.

In fact, the politicians took the last option and almost took the first option: the European Council appointed two members left of $SQ1$, one on $SQ1$, and three to the right of $SQ1$. They appointed Wim Duisenberg from the Netherlands as president; Christian Noyer from France as vice president; and Eugenio Domingo Solans from Spain, Sirkka Hämäläinen from Finland, Otmar Issing from Germany, and Tommaso Padoa-Schioppa from Italy as the other members.

If I assume, as before for the EMI Council members, that the five-year inflation rates of a country reflect the preferences of each board member from that country, the result is the configuration for the new Governing Council in Figure 5.4. The "2"s indicate that after the Executive Board appointments, two members are at a particular position. Both before and after the appointments, the status quo is the Dutch position at an inflation rate of 2.52 percent.

---

[51] PO: Portugal, SP: Spain, IT: Italy, FI: Finland, AU: Austria, IR: Ireland, FR: France, GE: Germany, BE: Belgium, LU: Luxembourg, and NE: Netherlands.

Figure 5.4: The New Governing Council after May 1998

Thus the veto power of the tight monetary policy countries combined with the current status quo ensured the continuation of the status quo. That status quo happened to coincide with relatively tight monetary policy. This simple model demonstrates how the institutional structure of the appointment process, essentially the unanimity rule for the Heads of States, together with the initial status quo favors tighter rather than easier monetary policy despite the entry of high-inflation countries. Given the status quo, Italy, Spain, and Portugal as well as Greece, will essentially have very little power in the appointment decisions.

Discussions regarding a larger EMU have neglected to deal with the institutional structure of the appointment process. Employing a mean inflation idea, discussions have assumed that the entrance of traditionally higher inflation countries will automatically increase inflation by raising the mean inflation rate. Some have argued that these higher inflation countries will put pressure on the ECB to lower interest rates. The model shows that this is a possibility (Case 1) but not in the context of the 1998 situation (Case 2). If the assumptions made here are reasonable and the initial status quo is for relatively tight monetary policy, then given the institutional structure of the appointment process, appointees to the Executive Board of the ECB will maintain tight monetary policy. In fact, the ECB has been criticized for relatively tight policy to date.

What would have happened if the Council of Ministers possessed the power to make binding proposals? Assume that the Council of Ministers would make such proposals using a qualified majority. Then Italy's ten-year average inflation rate of 5.14 percent is the qualified majority point. Based on the ordering of ten-year average inflation rates, Italy is the point at which the weighted votes exceed the qualified majority requirement (Table 5.4). But even with proposal power, the Council of Ministers would not have changed anything in the face of the veto power of the Heads of States to the right of the status quo; the equilibrium policy point would have remained at *SQ*1.

However, if the Council of Ministers only had to satisfy the median, it could have proposed France's indifference point, which would have

Table 5.4: *Voting Weights on the Council of Ministers*

	10-year Inflation	Voting Weights % of Total Council of Ministers Votes[a]	Cumulative Sum of Voting Weights
Netherlands	1.93	7.70	7.70
Luxembourg	2.34	3.10	10.80
Belgium	2.36	7.70	18.50
Germany	2.41	15.40	33.90
France	2.61	15.40	49.30
Ireland	2.69	4.60	53.90
Austria	2.72	6.20	60.10
Finland	3.33	4.60	64.70
Italy	5.14	15.40	80.10
Spain	5.30	12.30	92.40
Portugal	8.42	7.70	100.10

[a] I calculated these voting weights in the following manner. First, I calculated percent of total Council of Ministers votes for all fifteen EU countries. After omitting the non-initial-EMU countries of Denmark, Sweden, the UK, and Greece, I normalized the vote percentages of the remaining countries to 100.

Source: European Union; http://www.eu.int/inst/en/ep.htm#intro; IMF International Financial Statistics.

moved policy to the left of the median to about the location of Ireland's ideal point. Thus under this set of institutional arrangements with a Council of Ministers with binding proposal power and majority rule for the Heads of States, easier policy would have ensued. In effect, with a different set of institutions, the outcome would have been the feared outcome. With the set of adopted institutions, however, the fear was unjustified.

5.3.3 The Enlargement of the European Monetary Union

When Greece joined in 2001, the addition of Greece's national governor to the Governing Council moved $SQ1$ slightly from 2.52 percent to 2.60 percent – halfway between the Netherlands and Germany. Thus in Figure 5.3, there should be one more Head of State to the left of Portugal, and $SQ1$ should be slightly lower. Despite these changes, the case remained Case 2: deadlock.

Thus the Heads of States should have maintained $SQ1$. In 2002, the only appointment was for the vice chair position, held by Christian Noyer of France. The model predicts the appointment should have been to the right of the Netherlands in Figure 5.4 – the side of $SQ1$ on which France is located.

The prediction was almost right, but in the final outcome, it proved wrong. Belgium's Paul de Grauwe was a leading candidate, but he was beaten out by Greece's Lucas Papademos, which moved *SQ*1 from 2.60 percent to 2.68 percent – Germany's position. However, the difference between the model's predictions and the actual result is very slight – 0.08 percent – and the model's real verification or discreditation requires further observations.

The next round of appointments will be in 2003 with the replacements of Wim Duisenberg and Sirkka Hämäläinen. It is highly likely that Duisenberg will be replaced by Jean-Claude Trichet of France, and if not Trichet, another Frenchman. This appointment will not affect the median. Hämäläinen will be replaced by someone from a smaller country: Austria, Luxembourg, or Ireland. As long as Hämäläinen's replacement is not from Austria, this appointment should also not affect the median. Thus the model's predictions should be borne out by next year's appointments; policy should stay put at a relatively tight level.

The countries most likely to join in the next decade are the United Kingdom, Sweden, and the ten new EU countries as of 2004: Cyprus, the Czech Republic, Estonia, Hungary, Latvia, Lithuania, Malta, Poland, Slovakia, and Slovenia. Among all the countries under consideration, Sweden, the Czech Republic, Latvia, Estonia, and Lithuania look most likely to join sooner than later. The group may join in a wave together about three years from now. All have very good inflation records in the last five years and are unlikely to affect much the tightness of policy. The other countries are more problematic in terms of inflation records, but their membership looks set to come several years later.

5.4 SUMMARY

The EMU is still a relatively new phenomenon. In January of 1999, exchange rates were irrevocably fixed, and the ECB began to formulate monetary policy for eleven EU countries and for a twelfth in 2001. Who will be making policy? How will they be appointed? What does the structure of the process mean for the kind of resulting policy? These are the questions I have tried to answer in this chapter by applying a suitably modified appointment process model from Chapter 2.

The appointment process is driven by the veto power of each Head of State. In Case 1, when all the Heads of States are on one side of the status quo, policy change is possible. In Case 2, when at least one Head of State is on the other side of the statuo quo from the other Heads of States, policy change is impossible, and the status quo reigns.

In terms of the immediate future, the relevant questions are, are all the Heads of States located on one side of the status quo, and what does the status quo look like? In answer to the first question, there are some Heads of States on each side of the status quo – therefore, deadlock ensues. In answer to the second question, the status quo appears to favor relatively tight monetary policy. Thus the institutional structure of the appointment process seems to favor relatively tight monetary policy for the first few years of monetary union – even with the addition of Greece.

This runs counter to most discussions today regarding the possibility of a larger monetary union. The presumption in these discussions is that the inclusion of traditionally inflationary countries will necessarily lead to easy monetary policy. However, this chapter has shown that the institutional structure of the appointment process limits the influence of these countries given the circumstances.

The application has shown how different structures lead to different types of policies. In the Fed model, the circumstances can favor the president or the Senate median or the status quo. In the ECB process, the extreme Heads of States can dominate under certain circumstances, or the status quo will prevail. The policy outcomes are different due to two differences between the processes. First, there is no agenda setter; the Council of Minsters' proposals are not binding. Second, a unanimity rule characterizes the approval of the proposed nominees by the Heads of States. Those two differences have serious consequences for the types of policies produced under each setting. The conclusions in the final chapter suggest other possible applications and further discusses the implications of the different appointment structures.

6

The Origins of the Federal Reserve Appointment Process

In the previous chapters, the appointment process is exogenous; I take the process as given and explain how it affects policy. In this chapter, the appointment process is an endogenous object of choice – a dependent variable. I examine the development of the appointment process and claim that it is related to the centralization of the Federal Reserve System. Specifically, I compare and contrast the different appointment structures envisioned in the banking bills from 1903 to 1935.

6.1 THE THEORETICAL FRAMEWORK

6.1.1 *Assumptions and Definitions*

1. *The Dependent Variable: Appointment Power.* Appointment power is the extent to which the president and Senate can influence policy through appointments. It is related to the *appointment structure*, the structure of the appointment process and its effects on policy. The appointment structure's components are:

THE NUMBER OF APPOINTED MEMBERS. This variable refers to the number of members appointed by the president and Senate to the Fed's central decision-making board. On the FOMC, by appointing a larger proportion of the central board, the president and Senate have greater control over its decisions, because there is a greater likelihood that the FOMC median is one of their appointees. Because of political uncertainty, the president and Senate will not necessarily advocate a board composed totally of political appointees. With such a board, once in office, opponents can quickly reverse policy gains made by the current president and Senate.

THE LENGTH OF TERMS. This variable refers to how long each central board member serves. The longer the terms are, the greater the policy lock-in by politicians. But once in office, opponents will have the same advantage, and therefore, the politicians will not make terms too long.

THE FREQUENCY OF APPOINTMENTS. This variable refers to how often the president and Senate are allowed to make appointments. The more frequent the appointments are, the greater the policy influence is. Because of political uncertainty, politicians will often insulate the board by staggering appointment opportunities.

2. *The Independent Variable: Centralization.* Centralization is the extent to which the Federal Reserve Board between 1913 and 1935 and the FOMC since 1935 created and enforced monetary policy relative to the twelve district reserve banks. More specifically, I use the term to compare different proposals for the Fed: the National Reserve Association as envisioned in the Aldrich Bill of 1911, the Fed created in 1913, and the restructured Fed in 1935.

3. *The Actors.* The main actors are (1) various interest groups: bankers, Chambers of Commerce, and trade associations, and (2) parties: the Democrats and Republicans. The background section describes the actors more fully. I assume that the interest groups care about their respective businesses' long-term profitability and that the parties care about reelection and their legislative majorities.

6.1.2 *The Theory: Relating Centralization and Appointment Power*

Politicians can counteract decentralization by increasing appointment power – appointing a higher proportion of a board's members, lengthening appointment terms, and increasing the frequency of appointments.[52] In short, decentralization decreases the policy influence of politicians, but politicians can consolidate the remaining central authority through greater appointment power.

This study claims that the Fed's appointment structure resulted from political trade-offs between appointment power and centralization. In

---

[52] These three factors of appointment power have different potencies with respect to appointment power. In particular, as an anonymous referee pointed out, there is a linear relationship between term length and appointment power; doubling the terms leads to doubled delays in a president's ability to gain a majority on a board. However, doubling either board size or frequency does not have double the effect.

the Fed's creation in 1913, the Democrats traded the Republicans less centralization for more appointment power. Conversely, in the 1935 restructuring, the Democrats obtained less appointment power but more centralization.

6.2 BACKGROUND

6.2.1 The Pre-Federal Reserve Banking System

The pre-Fed era (before 1913) was characterized by a high frequency of severe economic panics. During the post–Civil War era, panics occurred approximately every ten years in 1873, 1884, 1890, 1893, and 1907 (Friedman and Schwartz 1963: 8). The last two panics preceding 1913 were the most severe, ultimately serving to galvanize efforts to reform the banking system.

The sequence of events for each panic was strikingly similar to that of the others. A failure of one bank would lead to runs,[53] then failures, of other banks. The problem was that because banks covered only a small proportion of their total liabilities in reserves, they could not cope with the sudden deluge of withdrawal requests. The drawdown of reserves then threatened to shut down the entire banking system. As a preventative measure, banks would temporarily suspend all payments (banking holidays). Lacking a payments system, the economy would slow down substantially.

The previously described snowball effects of a single bank failure were caused by the general instability of the banking system, which itself had three main causes: the pyramiding of bank reserves, no lender of last resort, and the inelasticity of the currency.

1. *Pyramiding of Bank Reserves.* The provisions of the National Banking Act of 1864 encouraged the pyramiding of reserves – a phenomenon in which smaller banks held reserves in medium-sized banks, who in turn held their reserves in large banks. The pyramiding of reserves increased the banking system's vulnerability to panics by providng the potential for one bank failure to draw down reserves in the entire banking system.

More precisely, the National Banking Act established the national banking system,[54] and allowed smaller national banks (also called *country*

---

[53] A bank run is a situation in which most bank depositors demand withdrawals of all their funds.

[54] The act defined national banks as those banks with a certain set of capital, reserve, and portfolio requirements that were higher than those of state banks.

banks) to maintain three-fifths of their reserves in other national banks (*city banks*) that were located in designated reserve cities. Later modifications allowed city banks to keep their reserves in New York's largest banks.

The National Banking Act's limitations on branch banking further promoted the pyramiding of assets. Because a bank could not operate beyond its local area, it could not expand and diversify its portfolio. Thus, most country banks' portfolios consisted of agricultural loans collaterized by land mortgages. Through city banks, country banks could invest excess reserves in the money market, thereby taking advantage of needed diversification. City banks also offered clearinghouse services, which allowed smaller banks to clear checks in a central location rather than dealing individually with one another (White 1983: 65–74). In turn, farther up the pyramid, city banks could place their reserves in the New York banks, thereby taking advantage of large clearinghouses, and through New York banks, city banks could invest their excess reserves in the stock market (White 1983: 28).

2. *No Lender of Last Resort.* A lender of last resort provides banks the liquidity necessary to meet the demands of its customers in times of crisis. Even more important than providing the actual cash on hand, the mere existence of a lender of last resort provides general confidence in the banking system.

The pre-Fed banking system lacked a true lender of last resort. Large private clearinghouse associations, especially the New York Clearinghouse Association, attempted to serve as lenders of last resort during the panics of 1857, 1860, 1893, and 1907.

Unfortunately, clearinghouse associations could not bear the system's load as the lender of last resort. The associations covered only a small proportion of the entire financial system because their stringent membership requirements excluded the growing number of different types of financial institutions. But when nonmember institutions failed, the credibility of member institutions was damaged. Thus clearinghouse associations sometimes bailed out nonmember institutions who had no incentive to play by the rules set by the clearinghouse associations. In the end, the associations could not afford to bail out all of the failing institutions.

3. *Inelasticity of the Currency.* Inelastic currency refers to the inability of the currency to expand and contract according to the needs of the economy. Currency inelasticity was a direct result of the National Banking

Act, which tied currency to government bonds. Because the number of government bonds increased according to the demands of fiscal policy rather than those of the economy, the act effectively fixed currency to fiscal policy.

The *demand* for currency, however, tended to increase seasonally and during panics. At the end of every summer, farmers required loans to harvest their crops and move them to market (Kettl 1986: 18). As for panics, they always resulted in a cash crunch for reserve drawdowns.

Whether season or panic related, sudden increases in currency demand required reserve withdrawals by banks, but the pyramiding of reserves restricted banks' abilities to recall their reserves. Thus together with the pyramiding of reserves, the inelasticity of the currency caused a number of major and minor panics.

Through monetary policy, a central bank could have alleviated problems caused by the sudden increased demand for currency by anticipating seasonal fluctuations in currency demand and increasing currency in the system through open market operations.[55] Open market operations are also an alternative or complementary method of injecting liquidity into the banking system during panics.

Realizing that this was the case, after fifty-five years of attempting to manage the system through private clearinghouses, most bankers agreed by the end of 1907 that some governmental steps were required to reform the banking system. Not surprisingly, they wanted to control the process of reform. However, the bankers were not a particularly cohesive group, as the next section describes.

6.2.2 *The Actors Behind Banking Reform*

1. The Bankers. By 1900 three distinct groups of bankers were interested in banking reform (Wiebe 1962: 24). The first group, country bankers, consisted of small, rural bankers whose banks' portfolios consisted mainly of agricultural and small business loans. The second group, city bankers, had portfolios with larger business loans and some financial market assets. The third group, *Eastern*, primarily *New York financiers*, dealt heavily in large business financing and loans to investors in the stock market.

---

[55] By buying domestic assets, a central bank increases the money supply because it buys those assets from banks and pays them with currency they create. By selling assets, a central bank decreases the money supply because it takes back some currency as payment for the assets.

These divisions among the bankers tended to be regional, with more country banks in the south and west, city bankers in the midwest (mainly in Chicago), and large financiers in the north and east.

These three groups fundamentally disagreed with one other regarding banking reform. The Eastern financiers wanted a central bank controlled by bankers and a currency backed by state, municipal, and railroad bonds, because they dealt often in such financial instruments. Both city bankers and country bankers feared that centralization meant control by the Eastern financiers at their expense. They also opposed a bond-backed currency because their dealings with such instruments were limited or nonexistent.

Although country bankers and city bankers agreed on decentralization and opposed a bond-backed currency, they disagreed with each other in other respects. The city bankers wanted to expand at the expense of country banks by proposing currency based on the liquid assets of a bank (generally nonmortgage and short-term commercial paper).[56] Because city banks tended to serve as reserve banks for smaller banks, they possessed liquid assets to a far greater degree than country banks who tended to hold agricultural and mortgage loans as assets. By proposing a currency based on the liquid assets of a bank, city bankers would have ensured control of the currency without interference from country banks.[57] Country banks would have backed an assets currency if the assets included agricultural credits, but city bankers' plans never included such assets. In addition to assets currency plans, city banks also tried to legalize branch banking, which was forbidden by the National Banking Act. Legalizing branch banking would have enabled city bankers to directly compete with country banks in their territory. Thus country banks strongly opposed branch banking.

These groups organized themselves into various banking associations. City bankers, particularly those from the midwest, dominated the largest of these organizations, the American Bankers' Association (ABA). However, country bankers controlled the state banking associations (Wiebe 1962: 24). Although country bankers were also members of the ABA, they seldom participated in its meetings, except to outvote the city bankers on very contentious issues such as the ABA's official position on pending congressional legislation. Eastern financiers never joined state

---

[56] Commercial paper usually constitutes short-term debt issues of large companies that can be bought and sold on the market.

[57] This idea was known as *assets currency.*

associations, and although some joined the ABA, they rarely participated in its activities. In promoting legislation, Eastern financiers usually worked separately from the ABA (Wiebe 1962: 24–5).

2. Other Business Interests. In 1908, the Boston Chamber of Commerce; the Merchants' Association and the Board of Trade and Transportation in New York; the Philadelphia Trades' League; the National Association of Credit Men; and other nonbanking business organizations formed the National Currency League. The purpose of the National Currency League was to protect the interests of businesses in banking reform. Although some businessmen supported central bank plans, many opposed such plans and preferred a decentralized system (Wiebe 1962: 76–9).

3. The Political Parties. The Republicans tended to back the interests of the powerful Eastern financiers, with whom some had close ties. Senator Nelson Aldrich, for example, had connections to the House of Morgan (Wiebe 1962: 75). The Republicans' earliest legislation on banking reform, not surprisingly, supported the existing private clearinghouse systems with the addition of the government as a lender of last resort.[58] Later legislation and the Republicans' platform for the 1912 election supported a central bank with the balance of the appointment power in favor of bankers.

Following the turn of the century, the Democrats provided far less leadership than the Republicans on the issue of banking reform. However, by the 1912 elections, the Democrats heavily attacked the Republican plans for a central bank by supporting a decentralized system with government appointment power. When they won the elections, the Democrats obtained the authority to set the banking reform agenda.

Bankers generally tended to support the Republicans, but country bankers and some city bankers defected to the Democrats' side during the debate over the Federal Reserve Act of 1913. The country bankers and half the city bankers fundamentally opposed a central bank, although they liked the idea of banker-controlled appointees. But they also feared, perhaps correctly, that those appointees would be controlled by Eastern financiers. Thus they tended to support the Democratic platform of a decentralized system with governmental appointees.

Table 6.1 summarizes the preferences of the actors with respect to the two dimensions of centralization and appointment power.

[58] The Aldrich-Vreeland Act of 1908.

Table 6.1: *Configuration of Interests in Banking Reform – Prior to 1913*

		Centralization	
		Low	High
Appointment Power	Low	Small minority of country bankers	Republicans Eastern and New York financiers Half of the city bankers Minority of business interests
	High	Democrats Majority of country bankers Half of the city bankers Majority of business interests	

6.3 THE CREATION OF THE FEDERAL RESERVE

The history of the Fed's creation and restructuring effectively illustrates the trade-offs between centralization and appointment power. In 1913, the Fed began as a decentralized institution in which regional reserve banks, rather than the central board, controlled the primary instrument of monetary policy – open market operations. The 1935 restructuring drastically centralized the Fed, placing most control of monetary policy in the newly created FOMC. However, with the centralization in 1935, elected officials lost appointment power. Whereas elected officials appointed all members of the central board prior to 1935, they appointed only seven of twelve members after 1935.

This section provides a detailed history of the Fed's creation and restructuring using the framework presented in Section 6.1. Sections 6.3.1 and 6.3.2 present the first legislative attempts undertaken by the Republicans. The Republican plans served as initial blueprints for the successful Democratic legislation presented in Sections 6.3.3 and 6.3.4.

6.3.1 *The First Legislative Attempts: The Republican Plans*

The first attempts to reform the banking system through legislative means began in 1903 with the Fowler Plan and Aldrich Plan, both Republican-sponsored bills. Rather than comprehensively reforming the banking system, the bills attempted to reshuffle interests in the current system.

1. *The First Fowler Bill (1903)*. The Fowler Bill supported city bankers' interests by legalizing an asset-backed currency and branch banking (Livingston 1986: 151–2). Due to the exclusion of agricultural credits from the list of assets and their opposition to branch banking, the country bankers did not support this bill. At the 1902 annual ABA meetings, country bankers succeeded in blocking a motion to support the Fowler Bill. However, ABA support was secured by some parliamentary trick (Wiebe 1962: 63; White 1983: 85–6). Country bankers subsequently used their state associations to issue resolutions in opposition to the bill and more significantly, they informed their congressional representatives of their opposition (Livingston 1986: 154).

Eastern financiers also opposed the bill. The then-current system of bond-backed currency worked to their competitive advantage because they had access to the bonds while other smaller banks, particularly city banks, did not. An asset-backed currency would have eroded this competitive advantage (Wiebe 1962: 64).

The two-pronged opposition by the country bankers and Eastern financiers doomed the Fowler Bill. The bill never made it out of the House.

2. *The First Aldrich Bill (1903)*. The Aldrich Bill of 1903 supported the interests of the New York and Eastern financiers. The bill allowed banks to form associations in times of crisis in order to issue emergency bond-backed currency, thereby legalizing the preexisting system of clearing-houses and their issuance of loan certificates during panics (White 1983: 88). The bill also allowed for a slight expansion of the assets on which currency was issued by including certain state, municipal, and railroad bonds (Wiebe 1962: 64). As with federal government bonds, Eastern financiers had ample access to these additional categories of bonds, while city and country bankers did not. In essence the bill did little other than to legitimize the status quo system of centralized reserves and currency issuance.

Not surprisingly, the New York and Eastern financiers heavily supported this bill and its sponsor, Senator Nelson Aldrich. The two other major banking groups, city and country bankers, opposed the Aldrich Bill mainly because of the bond-backed currency provisions. With two of the three major banking groups against the legislation, the Aldrich Bill, like the Fowler Bill, failed to pass.

3. *The Second Fowler Bill (1906)*. The midwestern city bankers again tried to introduce a carbon copy of the earlier Fowler Bill in 1906. As in the

earlier round, the country bankers effectively attacked the plan, and the second Fowler Bill of 1906 died in committee (Wiebe 1962: 64).

4. *Summary of the First Republican Bills.* Although none of the Republican plans passed, they mobilized interests with respect to the centralization of the banking system. In this context, centralization refers to the Eastern clearinghouse associations versus the regional banks' powers to control the money supply.

The legislative thrust came from either city bankers or Eastern financiers, but neither group's legislators were strong enough to win legislative battles without the support of legislators backed by the country bankers. Eastern financiers wanted to further legitimize the current centralized reserve and currency issuance system. City bankers wanted to decentralize that system by allowing for the issuance of currency on assets more accessible to them. Country bankers also wanted more decentralization, and they did not necessarily oppose the idea of an assets currency, but they would not endorse assets currency plans that did not include agricultural credits in the list of assets and that were connected with plans to legalize branch banking.

It should be pointed out that the split in interests described in this subsection occurred *within* the Republican party. In these earlier rounds of legislative banking reform, the Democrats tended to steer clear of the issue, having been severely defeated on the issue of silver-backed currency in the late nineteenth century.

6.3.2 *Bigger and Better Republican Plans*

1. *The Panic of 1907 and Renewed Reform Attempts.* A severe panic occurred in 1907, serving to galvanize further banking reform attempts. Just before the annual movement of crops, the European banks raised discount rates, and together with a downturn in the business cycle, these actions led to a severe credit and liquidity crunch in New York. When New York's second-largest trust company,[59] Knickerbocker Trust Company, suspended payments, this began a run on other financial institutions in New York. City and country bankers subsequently found that they could

---

[59] Trust companies began as firms that managed large trust funds for wealthy families. However, over time they began to offer services comparable to any bank: for example, loans and demand deposit accounts. Trust companies were not usually clearinghouse association members (White 1983: 38).

not draw on their New York balances, and they too had to suspend payments. To ease the situation, the Treasury intervened and deposited $25 million in the New York banks (White 1983: 77–8).

This chain of events convinced many that the financial system had grown beyond the abilities of the large clearinghouse associations to provide a remedy during panics. Knickerbocker was not a member of the New York Clearinghouse Association because it did not, nor did it desire, to meet the stringent membership requirements. But the solvency of nonmember institutions, like Knickerbocker, had a profound effect on the solvency of the entire financial system. Clearinghouse associations often had to bail out nonmember institutions in order to maintain confidence in the system. Essentially, the clearinghouse associations were providing a public good by assuming responsibility for the healthiness of the entire system, and the nonmember institutions were free-riding off this system. As the number of free-riders, nonmember institutions, grew, the largest clearinghouses had a difficult time controlling the system.

2. *The Second Aldrich Bill (1907).* Rather than comprehensive reform, the Aldrich Bill of 1907 was designed as a stop-gap measure to legalize and bolster, with Treasury funds, the actions of clearinghouse associations during panics. The bill was very similar to the 1903 Aldrich Bill, and like it, it was largely written to reflect the recommendations of the New York and Eastern financiers – this was their bill. The bill allowed any national bank to issue emergency currency upon approval by the Comptroller of the Currency and the deposit of state, municipal, or railroad bonds (Livingston 1986: 182).

The bill further stipulated the creation of a National Monetary Commission to study the problems of the banking system. The commission was to be composed of five members from each house of Congress and five members to be appointed by the president. No more than three of each set of five could be from the same party (*Congressional Record*, 60th Congress, 1st Session, pp. 1908–3852). Because the Republicans controlled both houses as well as the presidency, this scheme biased representation on the commission toward the Republicans.

Not surprisingly, the city and country bankers opposed the bill. Both groups objected to the railroad bond provision – the category of bonds to which New York and Eastern financiers had almost exclusive access. In response, the Senate amended the bill to eliminate the railroad bonds provision and managed to pass the bill. In the House, a still more compromising version of the Aldrich Bill passed: the Vreeland Act. The

Vreeland Act contained a local government bond provision that placated the city bankers but did not satisfy the country bankers. Eastern merchants and manufacturers also opposed the bill because it gave too much control to the large financiers. But with the support of city bankers and the Eastern financiers, the Republicans had enough support to pass the Aldrich-Vreeland Act of 1908 along partisan lines (*Congressional Record*, 60th Congress, 1st Session, pp. 7078, 7263).

3. The Third Aldrich Bill (1911). After four years, the National Monetary Commission produced the Aldrich Bill of 1911, a Republican bill designed to comprehensively reform the banking system. For the first time in the U.S. legislative history of banking reform, the Aldrich Bill included provisions for a new system of governmental institutions for regulating the banking industry. Compared to later bills, the Aldrich Bill provided for a relatively centralized institution and very little appointment power for elected officials.

a. Centralization and Appointment Power

a1. **Centralization: Medium.**[60] The Aldrich Bill would have created a centralized institution called the National Reserve Association. It was to consist of a central bank with fifteen branches. The central bank would have stored the capital of the member institutions of the National Reserve Association, dealt with open market operations, and set a uniform discount rate; thus the central bank would have had substantial powers over monetary policy.[61] Some decentralized power would have existed in the form of individual branches' right to rediscount paper, that is buy and sell commercial paper (Livingston 1986: 207).

a2. **Appointment power: Low.** Appointment power was to be in the district branches, and thus bankers, rather than politicians, would have controlled appointments.

a2(1) **Number of appointed members: five of forty-six.** The Aldrich Bill allowed elected officials to appoint only five of forty-six total

[60] Henceforth, high, medium, and low with respect to centralization and appointment power refer to relative comparisons among the three bills: the Aldrich Bill of 1911, the Federal Reserve Act of 1913, and the Banking Act of 1935.

[61] Discount policy has to do with the Fed's role as lender of last resort. Banks can borrow money from the Fed at the discount window at the discount rate. In practice borrowing by banks is done more frequently than in times of crisis, but the discount market constitutes a far smaller part of the money market than the federal funds market. Therefore, the premier decision-making body of the Federal Reserve System is the FOMC and not the BOG.

members on a *National Board of Directors*. The board would have consisted of thirty-nine directors, two from each district and nine chosen to represent stock holders,[62] and seven ex officio members, for a total membership of forty-six. The ex officio members were to consist of a governor (also the chairman of the board), two deputy governors, the Secretary of Agriculture, the Secretary of Treasury, the Comptroller of Currency, and the Secretary of Commerce and Labor. The president would have appointed the governor, but the directors, elected by the districts (the Elected Board), would have chosen the list of potential nominees. These same elected directors would have had the right to remove the governor with a two-thirds vote. The Elected Board would have chosen the two deputy governors who could be removed by a majority vote of the board. These latter provisions served to further limit the power of elected officials' appointees (West 1977: 74).

In addition, an *executive committee* would have consisted of nine members. The executive committee would most probably have been the working body of the association. Five members would have been chosen from the Elected Board in addition to the governor, the two deputy governors, and the Comptroller of Currency (West 1977: 74). As with the National Board of Directors, elected officials would have had the power to appoint very few members of the executive committee – only the governor and the Comptroller of Currency. However, due to the district directors' provision of the list of possible appointees, and the Elected Board's right to remove the governor, the president's power to appoint even the governor would have been, in fact, highly proscribed.

Because member banks would have elected the branches' board members, who in turn would have controlled forty-two of the forty-six members of the National Board of Directors and eight of the nine members of the executive committee, bankers would have heavily influenced the decisions of the National Reserve Association. With the dominance of the member banks, elected board members would have secured the dominance of the bankers over the government appointees.

a2(2) **Length of terms: three years.** All members of the board, except the Secretary of Agriculture, Secretary of Commerce and Labor,

---

[62] Member banks were required to purchase stocks of the National Reserve Association and were thus the true owners of the association.

Table 6.2: *Relative Comparisons of Significant Banking Reform Bills*

	Aldrich NRA Bill	Federal Reserve Act of 1913	Banking Act of 1935
Centralization	Medium	Low	High
Appointment Power	Low	High	Medium
(a) Number of appointments	5/46	7/7	7/12
(b) Length of terms	3 years	10 years	14 years
(c) Frequency of appointment opportunities	3 years	2 years	2 years

The entries high, medium, and low refer to relative comparisons among the three bills.
NRA: National Reserve Association

Secretary of Treasury, and Comptroller of Currency, were to serve three years (West 1977: 74). This gave a slight advantage to elected officials over the bankers because the secretaries often served four years. However, the nonelected officials' appointments so vastly outnumbered the elected officials' appointments as to completely negate this advantage.

a2(3) Frequency of appointments: every three years. No staggering of appointments was envisioned. Every three years, a whole new board would be in place. Normally, staggering matters for elected officials' abilities to appoint a substantial proportion of a central board; by limiting their abilities to appoint all members, staggering restricts the potential for influence through appointments. In this case, because elected officials would have had so little power to make appointments in the first place, the lack of staggering would not have affected their power over appointments.

Table 6.2 summarizes the provisions of the Aldrich Bill.

b. The Death of the Aldrich Bill

Even before its introduction in 1912, the Aldrich Bill[63] received quite a bit of negative publicity because of the National Reserve Association's similarity to a traditionally centralized central bank. The Democrats assisted in the negative publicity and used the general suspicion of the bill to their advantage. The Democrats captured the House in 1910 and shortly following the bill's introduction, the Democrats won the Senate and the presidency in the 1912 elections, partially

---

[63] Henceforth, references to the Aldrich Bill refer to the 1911 bill unless otherwise noted.

by emphasizing their opposition to the Aldrich Bill (Kettl 1986: 20). With the Democrats' achievement of unified government for the first time in twenty years, they controlled the future direction of banking reform – at least for the time being.

6.3.3 The Advent of the Federal Reserve System: The First Democratic Plan

Despite rejection by Congress, the Aldrich Bill set the starting point for banking reform. Following the Democratic victory in 1912, Carter Glass became chairman of the House Banking Committee's subcommittee on banking reform (Kolko 1967: 219). Basically inexperienced in banking affairs, Glass hired H. Parker Willis, an economist and former student of J. Laurence Laughlin. Laughlin was the head of the National Citizens' League, a branch of the ABA created to educate the public on the Aldrich Bill. Glass took the advice of Willis regarding the new banking reform bill, and not surprisingly, the eventual Federal Reserve Act closely resembled the Aldrich Bill. Both specified reserve systems with some powers given to reserve banks, although the Aldrich Bill would have created a much more centralized system.

1. The Federal Reserve Act of 1913. In drafting the Federal Reserve Act, Glass started with the Aldrich Plan and altered it to suit the interests of the Democratic party – by trading off less centralization for more appointment power.

a.   Centralization and Appointment Power
a1. Centralization: Low. The Glass Bill decentralized the reserve system, twelve reserve banks with a coordinating central body – the Federal Reserve Board – to a far greater extent than the Aldrich Bill would have. First, members of the Federal Reserve System were to keep their required capital in reserve banks rather than a central bank, as they would have in the National Reserve Association. Second, reserve banks could perform open market operations whereas the National Reserve Board would have controlled such operations. Third, reserve banks could set their own discount rates, and the Federal Reserve Board did not require them to be uniform throughout the system, as the National Reserve Board would have done. Fourth, more reserves could be kept in member banks' own vaults and in the reserve banks rather than in the central bank as required in the Aldrich Bill.

Fifth, reserve banks under both schemes could rediscount paper, but in the Federal Reserve Act, eligible paper included agricultural credits. This enabled reserve banks to lend money based on local agricultural conditions.

Despite giving considerable policy-making powers to regional reserve banks, the Federal Reserve Act also gave important powers to the Federal Reserve Board. Most significantly, although regional banks could rediscount paper, the board could require regional banks "to rediscount the discounted paper of other Federal reserve banks at rates of interest to be fixed by the Federal Reserve Board" (Federal Reserve Act §11[b]). Essentially, the board could coordinate the monetary actions of the several regional reserve banks. The board also had a variety of other powers such as the power to review regional reserve banks; suspend any of the act's provisions for thirty days; issue and retire Federal reserve notes; add reserve cities; and suspend or remove officers and directors of reserve banks (Federal Reserve Act §11[a]-[l]).

a2. Appointment power: High. Government appointees controlled the Federal Reserve Board.

a2(1) The number of appointed members: seven of seven. The president and Senate appointed all seven members of the Federal Reserve Board, which consisted of the comptroller of currency, secretary of the treasury, and five other members appointed by the president with the advice and consent of the Senate.

a2(2) Length of terms: ten years. Every noncabinet board member was to serve for ten years except for the first five members: "One shall be designated by the President to serve for two, one for four, one for six, one for eight, and one for ten years" (Federal Reserve Act §10). For the Democrats, this meant that despite possible losses in the 1914 midterm congressional elections, the next presidential election in 1916, and all other elections until 1923, they would still retain at least six board seats for three years, three seats for six years, two seats for eight years, and one seat for ten years. In other words, they would have had a majority representation for at least three years and a just-under-majority for at least six years.

a2(3) Frequency of appointments: every two years. The president and Senate could make appointments to the board every two years. Unless board members retired early, this meant that every administration could only make a maximum of two appointments, and each unaltered Senate could only make a maximum of one appointment.

Staggering appointment opportunities in this manner limited the potential of future Republican victories to quickly alter the policy composition of the board.

Table 6.2 summarizes the structural features of the 1913 Fed.

b. **Interest group opposition and support for the Glass Bill**

Opposition. Opposition to the Glass Bill was led by the large Eastern financiers and the half of the city bankers who supported the Republican Aldrich Bill. The large financiers especially opposed the government control provisions of the bill, because this cut directly into their current control of the banking system. They called for a banker-controlled system. Half of the city bankers also opposed government control and wanted a banker-controlled central bank. They too supported the Aldrich Bill and joined the Republican opposition to the Glass Bill (Wiebe 1962: 131).

Support. Support for the bill was provided by the other half of the city bankers and all of the country bankers. Those city bankers decided some legislation was better than none and supported the bill, although they too complained that the bill would lead to too much government control and too little centralization (Wiebe 1962: 131–2). Most of the country bankers supported the bill because they preferred government control to control by the large financiers. Many businessmen, especially small businessmen, supported the bill as well. Both the National Association of Manufacturers and the U.S. Chamber of Commerce supported portions of the bill. However, Wall Street businessmen generally opposed the bill. Table 6.1 lays out the configuration of interests.

c. **Passage of the bill**

From 1912 to 1913, the Pujo subcommittee of the House Banking Committee investigated the growing accumulation of financial interests in New York, the so-called "Money Trusts," epitomized by J.P. Morgan and his enterprises (Wiebe 1962: 78). The negative publicity generated by these hearings finally killed the Aldrich Bill, and convinced the Democrats, especially President Wilson, that their constituents wanted government control rather than banker control of a new banking system (West 1977: 122; Kettl 1986: 21).

With the sufficient support of their constituents (see Table 6.1), the Democrats passed the Federal Reserve Act on December 23, 1913. With a united government, the Democrats achieved everything they could hope for: both decentralization and government control.

Table 6.3: *Configuration of Interests in Banking Reform – 1935*

		Centralization	
		Low	High
Appointment Power	Low	Small minority of country bankers	*Aldrich NRA* *Bill – Republicans* Eastern and New York financiers Half of the city bankers Wall Street businessmen
	High	*Federal Reserve* *Act – Democrats* Majority of country bankers Half of the city bankers Small businessmen U.S. Chamber of Commerce National Association of Manufacturers Farmers	

6.3.4 Restructuring the Federal Reserve: The Second Democratic Plan

The Banking Act of 1935 drastically restructured the Federal Reserve system by making it much more centralized. However, in gaining centralization, elected officials lost some appointment power (see Tables 6.2 and 6.3).

1. *The Great Depression: The Context for Restructuring.* The new banking act primarily reflected the ideas of Marriner S. Eccles, a prominent Utah banker. Eccles believed that the Depression required expansionary fiscal policy, an idea very popular with the Roosevelt administration. According to Kettl, "[Eccles] was a Keynesian who had never heard of Keynes and who, in fact, publicly argued the virtues of compensatory fiscal policy before Keynes published his famous *General Theory*" (Kettl 1986: 47). His ideas greatly appealed to Roosevelt's administration, which soon began to float his name for the recently vacated Fed governor position.[64] Eccles,

---

[64] Before the passage of the 1935 act, the chairman of the Federal Reserve Board was called the "governor."

however, asked that major changes occur in the structure of the Fed before he considered the job (Kettl 1986: 48).

Eccles felt that three key problems plagued the Fed. First, its stated purpose was to accommodate the annual business cycles, but the Fed had no instructions with respect to periodic crises. Second, decentralization confused the issue of responsibility for monetary policy. Third, the Treasury influenced the Fed a great deal in its day-to-day operations because both the Secretary of the Treasury and the Comptroller of Currency held seats on the Federal Reserve Board, and the Secretary of the Treasury was the formal chairman of the Federal Reserve Board meeting, whenever he attended. In addition, the Federal Reserve Board had no facility of its own and was physically located in the Treasury. Especially during World War I, the Fed was often pressured to follow the Treasury's preferences in setting policy (Kettl 1986: 43)

These problems combined to produce disastrous results during the Depression. Without guidance and the power to make and effect unilateral decisions, the Fed did very little to alleviate the Depression. The Fed's inaction eventually worsened the Depression (Timberlake 1993: 266–9); its refusal to inject additional liquidity into the financial system meant that banks could not deal with the increasing cash crunch caused by bank runs, which were in turn exacerbated by failing businesses.

Eccles and Lauchlin Currie, one of Roosevelt's economic advisors, proposed a restructuring to deal with these three problems. First, the Fed would be given power to *actively promote* stable business conditions, rather than its previous mandate to *passively accommodate* business conditions.

Second, the system would be drastically centralized under the power of the BOG and the new FOMC. Discount policy would be designated the exclusive power of the BOG rather than that of the reserve banks. To further reduce reserve bank power, Eccles preferred no reserve bank representation on the new FOMC. The BOG would confirm the appointments of reserve bank presidents.

Third, the plan called for closer integration of monetary and fiscal policies. Kettl nicely sums up Currie's beliefs:

> Currie contended that the old arguments about the Fed's independence from the presidency were dangerous, and he argued, 'There is no economic problem more important than achieving and maintaining prosperity, and since the actions of the monetary authority have a direct bearing upon the strength of

business activity they must be subject to the control of the Administration.'
(Kettl 1986: 49).

Essentially it was the explicit purpose of the Democratic framers of
the bill to place the Fed under administration, that is Democratic control. According to Eccles' original plan, all members of the FOMC were
to be administration appointees, including the Treasury Secretary and
Comptroller of the Currency.

Eccles succeeded in obtaining a drastic centralization of the system,
but only at the cost of elected officials losing their complete control of
appointments in the central decision-making body. The restructured Fed
looked very similar to the Fed envisioned by Eccles but with some significant changes.

2. *The Banking Act of 1935*

a. Centralization and Appointment Power

a1. Centralization: High. The Banking Act of 1935 truly centralized the
powers over monetary policymaking. Previously regional banks could
set their own discount rates and perform open market operations. The
Banking Act transferred those powers to central bodies in the Federal
Reserve System. The power to set the discount rate was given to the
BOG, while the power to set open market operations policy was given
to the newly created FOMC. Through its control over open market operations, the FOMC has the power to set monetary policy by which the
regional reserve banks must abide. In addition, although the regional
banks' board of directors can elect their own bank presidents, their
election is subject to veto by the BOG.

That elected officials lost the ability to appoint all members of the
FOMC is quite significant. Although they retained the ability to appoint
all members of the BOG, the FOMC is, and was known to be, the more
important of the two because it has the power to determine open market
operations. Discount policy, which is determined by the BOG, is also
a component of monetary policy but a much smaller one compared to
open market operations.

a2. Appointment power: Medium. Centralization came at the cost of
lower appointment power.

**a2(1) Number of appointed members: seven of seven for the BOG,
seven of twelve for the FOMC.** Elected officials retained the power
to appoint all seven members of the BOG, but only managed to

obtain the power to appoint seven of the twelve members of the newly created FOMC, the remaining five being regional reserve bank presidents.

Eccles originally did not want the five regional reserve bank presidents on the FOMC. Their inclusion on the FOMC was part of a compromise in which he gained centralization of open market policy in the FOMC (Kettl 1986: 52).

a2(2) **Length of terms: fourteen years for the appointed members, one year for the reserve bank presidents.** The terms of appointed members were lengthened from ten to fourteen years. The members sitting on the BOG at the time of the bill's passage served out the remainder of their ten-year terms. These provisions meant that in addition to an appointment opportunity in 1934, if they won the 1936 election, the Democrats faced at least three more expiring terms in 1936, 1938, and 1940. In addition, because the Comptroller of Currency and the Secretary of the Treasury were no longer members of the BOG, and their seats were designated as appointed seats, the Democrats had two additional appointment opportunities. Therefore, between 1932 and 1940, the Democrats could appoint six of the seven presidential appointees of the FOMC, *and* most of these appointees had fourteen-year rather than ten-year terms. Because fourteen years spanned three and a half presidential administrations and seven sessions of congress, the Democrats had the ability to install their preferences over monetary policy in the FOMC for a long period of time.

Although reserve bank presidents serve on the FOMC, their influence is limited by their minority representation as well as their short one-year terms on the FOMC. All reserve bank presidents serve five-year terms at their respective reserve banks and one-year terms on the FOMC with the exception of the New York reserve bank president, who always sits on the FOMC.

a2(3) **Frequency of appointments: every two years.** Appointment opportunities are staggered such that they occur every two years. In theory this limits political influence because an administration has the ability to appoint a maximum of two members and each Senate can appoint only one member. Thus the initial appointment opportunities provided the Democrats the chance to pack the FOMC; the Republicans' influence would have been limited if they had won the 1940 election.

Table 6.2 summarizes the structural features of the Fed according to the Banking Act of 1935.

b. Passage of the bill

The Roosevelt administration sent the bill to the House, where it was introduced by Representative Henry Steagall. As a senator, Carter Glass, now the chairman of the Senate Committee on Banking and Currency, was not consulted in the drafting of the bill. Although he packed committee hearings with bankers who feared political control of the Fed, Glass and his committee members unanimously provided a favorable report, albeit with an amendment that removed the Treasury Secretary and the Comptroller of the Currency from the BOG and added the five reserve bank presidents to the FOMC (*Congressional Record*, 63rd Congress, 1st Session, p. 11777–8). Large financiers bitterly opposed the bill, but a coalition of other bankers, similar to that in 1913, supported the bill (Kettl 1986: 51–2)(see Table 6.3). Eccles and the administration opposed the amendment to the bill on the FOMC composition but accepted it as a part of the larger compromise in which the Fed was highly centralized.

After conference sessions, the bill passed on August 23, 1935. Essentially Eccles and the administration obtained almost everything they had hoped for. Eccles subsequently became chairman of the new BOG and FOMC, and promptly instituted easier monetary policy in line with the needs of the New Deal (Kettl 1986: 54–5).

Although Kettl places more weight on the informal relationship between Eccles and Roosevelt during Eccles' term as chair, the new structural arrangements in fact institutionalized greater control of monetary policy by elected officials. Presidential appointees outnumbered reserve banks seven to five on the FOMC. In addition, the BOG, made up exclusively of presidential appointees, could veto appointments of reserve bank presidents. Finally, the new FOMC, dominated by presidential nominees, had greater control than ever before over the twelve reserve banks and over monetary policy.

6.4 SUMMARY

Banking reform in the United States between 1903 and 1935 was characterized by trade-offs between centralization and appointment power. The first attempts at banking reform were dominated by Republicans. The various banking groups worked through the Republicans, with the New York and Eastern financiers gaining the most representation. In general, bankers were Republicans. But due to their distrust of New York bankers, the country bankers sometimes sided with the Democrats. When the Democrats swept both houses of Congress and the presidency in 1912, the control over banking reform shifted in a different direction toward less centralization and more appointment power by elected officials.

With the exception of small minority groups, both parties and their banking and business constituents favored some sort of reform by 1912. However, they disagreed on the exact nature of the reform. Debates on banking reform focused on two dimensions: the degree of centralization and degree of appointment power by elected officials. Republicans, backed by large financiers, favored a central bank under banker control. Directly opposed to the Republicans, the Democrats, backed by country bankers and business, favored a decentralized system under control of elected officials. With their political domination, Democrats passed the Federal Reserve Act of 1913, which established a decentralized system with substantial appointment power by elected officials.

In 1935, Depression politics made the Democrats realize that they needed to effectively control monetary policy in order to stimulate the economy with various government plans. They succeeded in drastically centralizing the system but at the cost of appointment power. The newly created FOMC completely controlled monetary policy, but elected officials could no longer appoint all members of the central board.

7

Conclusions

When Clinton nominated Edward Gramlich and Roger Ferguson to the BOG in the fall of 1997, the Senate reaction was notable for its absence. In stark contrast to the critical attack on Rohatyn, the senators barely commented on these nominations except to praise the nominees' "extraordinary backgrounds" (Senator D'Amato, Chairman of the Senate Banking Committee, quoted in Wessel 1997: A10). The hearings were short, and the full Senate voted quickly to appoint Gramlich and Ferguson.

Clinton had learned a great deal from the Rohatyn nomination. He had discovered that Rohatyn was too far on the easy side relative to what the Senate would tolerate. Perhaps even Rivlin was a bit problematic; the Senate's confirmation vote on her appointment was not unanimous – a rare occurrence. Clinton needed to nominate someone like Meyer, who supported the current Fed policy and thus seemed likely to be a future median member of the FOMC. According to this criterion, Gramlich and Ferguson were good choices. At the time of their confirmation hearings, the FOMC was split into two factions; one side expected an imminent inflation rise while the other side claimed the possibility of a golden age with continued low inflation and high growth. In the hearings, Gramlich and Ferguson both staked a middle position with neither taking sides in the FOMC debate. Satisfied with this anticipated choice by Clinton, the Senate approved both the nominees.

This story bolsters the claims made in this study: that politicians appoint with an eye toward policy and that both the president and the Senate may matter in the appointment process. But like the Rohatyn anecdote, it too is just another supporting story. The purpose of this study has been to generalize the claims made from the anecdotes. With this aim in mind, the study began with three questions and now ends with three answers.

139

Conclusions

Question 1: Do politicians influence monetary policy through appointments to the Federal Reserve? The answer is "yes" – that the results support influence. I developed a formal model of the appointment process that predicted the location of policy following every appointment; the model specified the exact constraints of the process. I then developed a new method to estimate monetary policy preferences and used the resulting estimates to empirically test the model's predictions. In approximately 87–91 percent of the FOMC cases and 91–100 percent of the BOG cases, the median changed as predicted by the model. Furthermore, the results support political influence on actual policy; the model predicts the FOMC's federal funds rate about 33 percent of the time and the BOG's discount rate about 38 percent of the time.

Thus despite the sometimes widely acclaimed, and at other times widely criticized independence of the Fed, appointments are an important avenue of political influence on the Fed. Returning to this book's opening paragraphs, independence does not mean absolute independence from political authority. Politicians may delegate monetary policy powers to the Fed, but they have never taken a completely hands-off attitude toward it. Appointments constitute one of the ways in which politicians maintain some control over the Fed and its policies.

As this study has shown, appointments are neither a quick nor a surefire way to influence the Fed. For either the president or the Senate to obtain their desired policy, it usually takes both time and luck because the right seats must become vacant at the right time for influence to occur in the desired direction. For example, when the president and Senate are far left of the status quo, a vacancy in the last five seats produces the largest policy change toward their ideal points. Timing matters because if the vacancy occurs when the president is closer to the status quo, his ideal point may be the outcome, whereas if the Senate is closer, the outcome will be more favorable toward the Senate.

But rather than luck, perhaps the locations of the vacancies also have a general logic. From a cursory look at the twenty-three appointments from the study, it seems that sometimes members leave when they become the extreme members of the FOMC. For instance, when Volcker entered the Fed among Carter appointees in 1979, he was a moderate compared to the other FOMC members. When he left in 1987, he did so as the strongest inflation hawk in a largely Reagan-appointed FOMC. Perhaps an extreme member feels alone and frustrated on an FOMC that does not pay attention to her preferences, and which is, in her view, changing inhospitably with each appointment. This remains a possible topic for future research.

Question 2: Who influences appointments to the Fed? The answer is sometimes just the president, sometimes both the president and Senate, and sometimes neither. Although the president is alert to the Senate's wishes at all times, sometimes he does not have to pay attention to the Senate's preferences, while at other times, he really must. It depends on the situation: whether the president and Senate agree on the direction of policy change, and where the president and the Senate are located on the monetary policy dimension relative to one another and the current policy. There are times when both agree on the direction in which policy should move, but either the president or the Senate is closer to the current policy. The closer party then decides just how far policy will move. At other times, they do not even agree on the direction of policy. In that case, they deadlock and maintain the current policy.

But does the president always dominate? The answer to this question is "no" for the FOMC and "maybe" for the BOG. The results supported both the influence of the president and Senate on the FOMC, while the results for the BOG were inconclusive.

In any case, the results do support dominance within an anticipation framework. In the model and analysis presented here, the president always anticipates the Senate. Even within that anticipation framework, the model showed that the Senate can be completely powerless against a president, often because of the president's agenda-setting power. While the vice versa is never true, the president nevertheless sometimes has to compromise with the Senate. Thus there is sometimes presidential dominance and sometimes presidential compromise, all within presidential anticipation. Thus the resolution of the debate between the presidential anticipation and presidential dominance theories is that even when anticipation is always the case, dominance can occur within anticipation under the specified conditions.

In these results, the intent of the Constitution's Framers is clearly realized. No branch fully dominates this process, demonstrating the functioning of the checks-and-balances system. However, the extent to which certain situations occur and to which one branch has influence over another in those situations will, more likely than not, vary across agencies. This possibility is suggested in Bailey and Chang's (1999) analysis of Supreme Court appointments. In that model, for any given spatial configuration, the influence of one branch over another depends on the costs of another round of nominations and confirmations. For example, if the president wishes to influence long-term policy and elections are approaching, it is better for him to appoint someone now rather than later unless he is certain of reelection. Thus, costs may be high for him in this situation. In the Senate, the cost of a major confirmation battle may be in terms of the time lost on other legislation. Beyond the Supreme Court and across agencies, these costs may vary. Certainly there are appointments over which the president seems to have more control such as cabinet appointments. Likewise, the Senate seems to control other appointments such as lower-court appointments. A comparative study across agencies, like McCarty and Razaghian's (1999) study of confirmation times, may shed more light on these considerations.

An alternative comparative route is to go across countries rather than across American agencies. As mentioned in the introduction, countries vary quite a bit in terms of how they appoint their central bankers. In some countries, the executive branch has complete power to appoint, and in others, the legislative branch has that power. Sometimes the two share the power with one party nominating and the other confirming the appointment. From a cursory view, it seems that in parliamentary systems, either the legislature or the cabinet appoints (e.g., Sweden, Japan), and in separation of powers systems, the power is left up to the executive branch (e.g., Australia). But still, there are exceptions to this rule. In the United States, the president shares the power with the Senate. Germany is a mixed system and has elements of both; some members are appointed by the president upon nomination by the cabinet, while others are appointed by the president upon nomination by the Bundesrat. A comparative study of appointment processes would yield some interesting insights into whether this conjecture regarding governmental systems and processes holds up. It may also shed light on whether these systematic differences in process affect the existence and level of political influence on policy: the answer to this book's first question.[65]

Question 3: What explains the current appointment structure of the Federal Reserve? The answer is greater centralization. I conducted detailed qualitative comparisons of the important Fed-related legislation during the period 1903–35. I found that in 1913, the Democrats obtained much appointment power and not much centralization. In 1935, the last major restructuring of the Fed, the Democrats sacrificed appointment power for greater centralization. Specifically, they gave up the ability to appoint

---

[65] Moser (1997) shows in a comparative study that central bank independence only solves the time inconsistency problem when legislative systems have two veto players as in a bicameral system.

all members of the central board, the FOMC, for the centralization of open market operations in the FOMC. The result was a more coherent, powerful Federal Reserve, which meant that the president's remaining appointees to the FOMC would have greater influence on policy than previously.

This question would also benefit from a comparative investigation, both across American agencies and across countries. Across agencies, there is a great deal of variation in the degree to which policy is centralized. Take the examples of the Occupational Safety and Health Administration (OSHA) and the National Labor Relations Board (NLRB). In the former, OSHA creates the national standards but allows states the power to enforce those standards. In the latter, the NLRB's central board controls both policy making and enforcement. Similarly, the agencies vary in appointment power. With regard to the number of appointees on the central board, OSHA has one – the Assistant Secretary of Labor for OSHA – while the NLRB has five board members. With regard to term lengths, the Assistant Secretary of Labor for OSHA serves at the pleasure of the president. The NLRB's members serve for five years. In terms of the frequency of appointments, the president really controls this for OSHA. The NLRB appointment opportunities occur every year. Thus the structures of these two agencies are quite different, despite their both dealing with workers' rights to some extent. OSHA is less centralized but the president and Senate have higher appointment power compared to the NLRB, which is more centralized. The comparison between the two holds up the theory presented in this study regarding the trade-offs between centralization and appointment power, but real support for the theory awaits further cross-sectional evidence.

Across countries, the structure of central banks varies greatly although not in terms of centralization; most are highly centralized with the branches having little to no power to determine monetary policy. Most of the variation occurs in terms of appointment power. The Bundesbank has up to seventeen members on its central board, eight of whom are appointed by the federal government. The Bank of Japan's central board has nine members, all of whom are appointed by the federal government. The Bank of Japan's directors serve five years, while the Bundesbank's members serve eight years. Therefore, the Japanese federal government can influence the Bank of Japan in greater proportion and more often compared to the German federal government in the Bundesbank setup. In this comparison, centralization does not vary much, but appointment power does; it seems to be higher in Japan compared to Germany.[66] As with the question of who influences, the governmental system may explain the differences in appointment power. In a parliamentary system like Japan, the principle of government is to give power to those in power; thus there is greater potential for quick political influence through appointments in Japan. In a separation of powers system, like parts of the German system, the opposite principle prevails, a principle of balance between the branches and influence by them together. The latter may lead to a process in which it is more difficult to influence the central bank through appointments.

Adapting the model. In addition to studying these three questions cross-sectionally across American agencies and/or across countries, the approach used in this study can be applied to a series of appointments within a specific agency or country over time. The methodological approach used in this study has been comprehensive. I started with an anecdotal observation: appointments seem to affect policy. I then used a formal model to logically derive if and how appointments could affect policy within the institutional constraints provided by the American constitutional system. The model yielded testable predictions based on the spatial configuration of the actors' preferences. The next logical step was to estimate the actors' preferences by using methods suited to the particular problems of the data. I therefore developed a new method that controls for swings in the business cycle and produces estimates that are comparable across the president, Senate, and the FOMC. I then used these preference estimates to test the model's predictions. I next looked into whether or not the process under study was the result of political intention. For this analysis, I used comparative case-study methods by looking at several variables across different legislative bills and acts.

The approach developed is a start-to-finish way of looking at interbranch interaction not only in the American system, but in other systems as well. The details will vary, but the general problem will not. In any system, there will be strategic interaction between different institutional actors with heterogenous preferences. In the ECB, for example, the sequence of the appointment process is similar to the nomination/confirmation sequence in the American system. However, the actors and their powers are very different. The Council of Ministers does not have the power to make

---

[66] Some of these considerations are discussed at length by Lohmann (1997) with respect to the Bundesbank.

binding commitments like the president of the United States. The Heads of States must unanimously accept a nominee whereas the Senate has only to approve a nominee by majority vote. As Chapter 5 showed, these differences have important implications for the types of policies produced in each setting. In the United States, politicians who represent median interests gradually move policy through appointments. In the European setting, either extreme countries dominate policy, or the current policy is extremely hard to change.

The results in Chapter 5 lend some, but not absolute, support for the concerns surrounding the entry of traditionally inflationary countries like Italy, Spain, and Portugal (Coleman 1998; Kosters, et al. 1998). These countries were seen as possible threats to economic convergence and the stability of EMU. But the arguments against the entry of these countries was based on an idea of a mean monetary policy among the EMU member countries: for example, if Italy joins, it automatically decreases the mean stability and increases the mean inflationary policy. As such, these arguments neglected the appointment process and its possible effects on policy.

Through an analysis of the appointment process, Chapter 5 has shown that the entry of these countries *could* lead to inflationary policy under certain conditions but that it is not a foregone conclusion. If a current policy is relatively different from the preferences of all the member countries, then the preferences of an extreme country, as Italy has been labeled, may dominate. But did these conditions exist at the start of EMU? The answer is "no". The latter part of Chapter 5 demonstrated that the pre-EMU European monetary policy and the countries' preferences dictated the continuation of the status quo – relatively tight monetary policy. Thus the entrance of Italy, Spain, and Portugal did not contribute to more inflationary policy in the first few years of EMU.

We can also use this approach to look in detail at other appointments in the American system. In Bailey and Chang (1999, 2001, 2003), we use a similar model to examine Supreme Court appointments. The basic process is the same as that for the Fed: presidential nomination followed by Senate confirmation. There are, however, differences that affect whether influence occurs and who is influential. The first difference is the time lag between appointments. Supreme Court appointments occur infrequently relative to Fed appointments. For the latter, presidents are guaranteed at least one appointment every other year. In contrast, there are no guarantees for Supreme Court appointments; presidents have to wait for deaths or retirements that can take many years. In the Supreme Court setting, politicians can never be sure that there will be further appointment opportunities that will get them closer to the RR equilibrium policy. Second, Supreme Court appointments are made to another major branch of government and have life terms. They are therefore very high-profile and highly publicized appointments compared to Fed appointments.

In such a setting, one might expect greater conflict between the president and Senate compared to the Fed appointment setting. Because each appointment is rare and high profile, it may be more important for both the president and Senate to obtain exactly what they each want. We allow for this conflict through the different costs that either party bears in the case of a repeat-nomination process. Preliminary results indicate that political influence occurs but perhaps not to the extent that it does for the Fed.

These are only two examples, but they illustrate how the approach from this book can be flexibly adapted to different governmental systems and to different appointment settings within the American system. Making these sorts of detailed comparisons is important to our understanding of how different institutional structures lead to different types of policy outcomes. Comparing the Fed and the ECB, we saw that the ECB structure is more likely to yield extreme policies or no change in policy at all. In comparisons of the Fed and the Supreme Court, perhaps politicians are unable to influence the Supreme Court through appointments as effectively as the Fed. What other differences will reveal themselves from a further investigation of other appointment processes remains to be seen.

With this understanding of the relationship between institutions and outcomes, there is also a normative implication. If we know the mapping from structures to outcomes, and if society can decide what type of policy it wants, then it can implement the correct structures for the correct types of policies. But making normative statements was never the intent of this book; that's a topic for another book altogether.

Bibliography

Alesina, Alberto. 1987. Macroeconomic Policy in a Two-party System as a Repeated Game. *Quarterly Journal of Economics* 102: 651–78.

Alesina, Alberto and Victor Grilli. 1992. The European Central Bank: Reshaping Monetary Politics in Europe. In Canzoneri, Grilli, and Masson, eds., *Establishing a Central Bank: Issues in Europe and Lessons from the U.S.* Cambridge: Cambridge University Press.

Alesina, Alberto and Howard Rosenthal. 1995. *Partisan Politics: Divided Government and the Economy.* Cambridge: Cambridge University Press.

Alesina, Alberto and Nouriel Roubini. 1990. Political Cycles in OECD Economies. *Review of Economic Studies* 59: 663–88.

Alesina, Alberto and Lawrence Summers. 1993. Central bank independence and macroeconomic performance: Some comparative evidence. *Journal of Money, Credit and Banking* 25: 151–62.

Bailey, Michael and Kelly Chang. 1999. Influencing the Court: A Formal and Empirical Analysis of Supreme Court Appointments. Paper presented at the 1999 Annual Meeting of the Midwest Political Science Association.

Bailey, Michael and Kelly Chang. 2001. Comparing Presidents, Senators, and Supreme Court Justices: Inter-institutional Preference Estimation. *Journal of Law, Economics and Organization* 17(2): 477–506.

Bailey, Michael A. and Kelly H. Chang. 2003. Extremists on the Court: The Inter-Institutional Politics of Supreme Court Appointments. Paper presented at the 2003 Annual Meeting of the American Political Science Association, Philadelphia.

The Banking Act of 1935. Ch. 614, 49 Stat 684.

Bank of Japan Law. 1997.

Barro, Robert J. and David B. Gordon. 1983. A Positive Theory of Monetary Policy in a Natural Rate Model. *Journal of Political Economy* 91: 589–610.

Bawn, Kathleen. 1997. Choosing Strategies to Control the Bureaucracy: Statutory Constraints, Oversight, and the Committee System. *Journal of Law, Economics, and Organization* 13(1): 101–26.

Bayoumi, Tamim and Barry Eichengreen. 1996. Operationalizing the Theory of Optimum Currency Areas. *CEPR Discussion Paper Series, International Macroeconomics, No. 1484* October.

Beck, Nathaniel. 1982a. Presidential Influence on the Federal Reserve in the 1970s. *American Journal of Political Science* 26: 415–45.

Beck, Nathaniel 1982b. Parties, Administrations and American Macroeconomic Outcomes. *American Political Science Review* 26: 83–93.

Belden, Susan. 1989. Policy Preferences of FOMC Members as Revealed by Dissenting Votes. *Journal of Money, Credit, and Banking* 21: 432–41.

Blinder, Leaving Fed, Says Central Bank Should be More Open. *The Wall Street Journal* January 18, 1996: A6.

Board of Governors of the Federal Reserve System. *The Federal Reserve Bulletin.* Various volumes and issues.

Borins, Sanford F. 1972. The Political Economy of the Fed. *Public Policy* 20: 175–98.

Broz, J. Lawrence. 1997. *The International Origins of the Federal Reserve System.* Ithaca, NY: Cornell University Press.

Calvert, Randall L., Mathew D. McCubbins, and Barry R. Weingast. 1989. A Theory of Political Control and Agency Discretion. *American Journal of Political Science* 33: 588–611.

Cameron, Charles. 2000. *Veto Bargaining: Presidents and the Politics of Negative Power.* Cambridge: Cambridge University Press.

Cameron, Charles M., Albert D. Cover, and Jeffrey A. Segal. 1990. Senate Voting on Supreme Court Nominees: A Neoinstitutional Model. *American Political Science Review* 84(2): 525–34.

Cameron, Trudy Ann and Daniel D. Huppert. 1991. Referendum Contingent Valuation Estimates: Sensitivity to the Assignment of Offered Values. *Journal of the American Statistical Association* 86(416): 910–17.

Canterbery, E. R. 1967. A New Look at Federal Open Market Voting. *Western Economic Journal* 6: 25–38.

Canzoneri, Matthew B., Vittorio Grilli, and Paul R. Masson, eds. 1992. *Establishing a Central Bank: Issues in Europe and Lessons from the U.S.* Cambridge: Cambridge University Press.

Chang, Kelly H. 2001a. The President versus the Senate: Appointments in the American System of Separated Powers and the Federal Reserve. *Journal of Law, Economics, and Organization* 17(2): 319–55.

Chang, Kelly H. 2001b. Estimating Monetary Policy Preferences: Controlling for Economic Conditions in Preference Estimation. Unpublished working paper.

Chang, Kelly H. 2001c. Forecasting Fed Behavior. Unpublished working paper.

Chappell, Henry W., Thomas M. Havrilesky, and Rob Roy McGregor. 1993. Partisan Monetary Policies: Presidential Influence Through Power of Appointment. *Quarterly Journal of Economics* 108: 185–218.

Chappell, Henry W., Thomas M. Havrilesky, and Rob Roy McGregor. 1995. Policymakers, Institutions, and Central Bank Decisions. *Journal of Economics and Business* 47: 113–36.

Chappell, Henry W., Rob Roy McGregor, and Todd Vermilyea. 1998. Models of Monetary Policy Decision-Making: Arthur Burns and the Federal Open Market Committee. Paper presented at the 1998 Annual Meeting of the Midwest Political Science Association. March 30, 1998.

Bibliography

Chubb, John E. and Paul E. Peterson, eds. 1989. *Can the Government Govern?* Washington, DC: Brookings Institution.

Coase, Ronald. 1937. The Nature of the Firm. *Economica* 4: 386–405.

Coleman, Brian. 1998. Italy's Admission to the EMU Clique Depends on Overcoming German Fears. *The Wall Street Journal* February 17, 1998.

Congressional Record. 1908. 60th Congress, 1st Session.

Congressional Record. 1935. 73rd Congress, 1st Session.

Cukierman, Alex. 1992. *Central Bank Strategy, Credibility, and Independence.* Cambridge, MA: MIT Press.

Davidson, Russell and James G. Mackinnon. 1993. *Estimation and Inference in Econometrics.* NY: Oxford University Press.

A Diary for 1998. *The Economist* January 3, 1998: 20–1.

Dodd, Lawrence C. and Bruce I. Oppenheimer, eds. *Congress Reconsidered.* 4th ed. Washington, DC: Congressional Quarterly Press.

Dodd, Lawrence C. and Richard L. Schott. 1979. *Congress and the Administrative State.* NY: John Wiley and Sons.

Epstein, David L. and Sharyn O'Halloran. 1999. *Delegating Powers: A Transaction Cost Politics Approach to Policy Making under Separate Powers.* Cambridge: Cambridge University Press.

Erikson, Robert. 1990. Economic Conditions and the Presidential Vote: A Review of the Macrolevel Evidence. *American Journal of Political Science* 34: 373–99.

Eskridge, William and John Ferejohn. 1992. Making the Deal Stick: Enforcing the Original Constitutional Structure of Lawmaking in the Modern Regulatory States. *Journal of Law, Economics, and Organization* 8: 165–89.

European Commission. 1998. *Convergence Report: Prepared in Accordance with Article 109j(1) of the Treaty.* Brussels: European Commission, March 25, 1998.

Fair, Ray C. 1978. The Effect of Economic Events on Votes for President. *The Review of Political Science* 60: 159–73.

Faust, Jon. 1996. Whom Can We Trust to Run the Fed? Theoretical Support for the Founders' Views. *Journal of Monetary Economics* 37: 267–83.

Federal Reserve Act. 12 U.S.C.; ch. 6, 38 Stat. 251.

Ferejohn, John and Charles Shipan. 1990. Congressional Influence on Bureaucracy. *Journal of Law, Economics, and Organization* 6: 1–43.

Ferejohn, John A. and Charles R. Shipan. 1989. Congressional Influence on Administrative Agencies: A Case Study of Telecommunications Policy. In *Congress Reconsidered*, 4th ed., L.C. Dodd and B.I. Oppenheimer, eds. Washington, DC: Congressional Quarterly Press.

Frey, Bruno S. and Friedrich Schneider. 1981. Central Bank Behavior: A Positive Empirical Analysis. *Journal of Monetary Economics* 7: 291–315.

Friedman, Milton and Anna J. Schwartz. 1963. *A Monetary History of the United States, 1867–1960.* Princeton: Princeton University Press.

Full Employment and Balanced Growth Act of 1978. 92 Stat. 1897.

Gildea, John. 1990. A Theory of Open Market Committee Voting Behavior. In *The Political Economy of American Monetary Policy*, Thomas Mayer, ed. Cambridge: Cambridge University Press.

Greene, William H. 1993. *Econometric Analysis.* 2nd ed. New York: Macmillan.

Greider, William. 1987. *Secrets of the Temple: How the Federal Reserve Runs the Country.* New York: Simon and Schuster.

Grier, Kevin B. 1987. Presidential Elections and Federal Reserve Policy: An Empirical Test. *Southern Economic Journal* 54(2): 475–86.

Grier, Kevin B. 1991. Congressional Influence on U.S. Monetary Policy: An Empirical Test. *Journal of Monetary Economics* 28: 201–20.

Grilli, Vittorio, Donato Masciandro, and Guido Tabellini. 1991. Political and Monetary Institutions and Public Financial Policies in the Industrial Countries. *Economic Policy* October: 342–92.

Groseclose, Tim, Steven D. Levitt, and James M. Snyder, Jr. 1999. Comparing Interest Group Scores across Time and Chambers: Adjusted ADA Scores for the U.S. Congress. *American Political Science Review* 93(1): 33–50.

Hammond. Thomas H. and Jeffrey S. Hill. 1993. Deference of Preference? Explaining Senate Confirmation of Presidential Nominees to Administrative Agencies. *Journal of Theoretical Politics* 5: 23–59.

Hammond, Thomas H. and Jack H. Knott. 1996. Who Controls the Bureaucracy?: Presidential Power, Congressional Dominance, Legal Constraints, and Bureaucratic Autonomy in a Model of Multi-Institutional Policymaking. *Journal of Law, Economics, and Organization* 12(1): 119–66.

Hastings, Delbert C. and Ross M. Robertson. 1962. The Mysterious World of the Fed. *Business Horizons* Spring.

Havrilesky, Thomas. 1988. Monetary Policy Signaling from the Administration to the Federal Reserve. *Journal of Money, Credit and Banking* 20(1): 83–101.

Havrilesky, Thomas. 1991. The Frequency of Monetary Policy Signaling from the Administration to the Federal Reserve. *Journal of Money, Credit, and Banking* 23: 423–8.

Havrilesky, Thomas. 1993. *The Pressures on Monetary Policy.* New York: Kluwer.

Havrilesky, Thomas. 1995. *The Pressures on Monetary Policy.* 2nd ed. New York: Kluwer.

Havrilesky, Thomas and John Gildea. 1991. The Policy Preferences of FOMC Members as Revealed by Dissenting Votes. *Journal of Money, Credit and Banking* 23(1): 130–8.

Havrilesky, Thomas and John Gildea. 1992. Reliable and Unreliable Partisan Appointees to the Board of Governors. *Public Choice* 73(4): 397–417.

Havrilesky, Thomas and Robert Schweitzer. 1990. A Theory of FOMC Dissent Voting with Evidence from the Time Series. In *The Political Economy of American Monetary Policy*, Thomas Mayer, ed. Cambridge: Cambridge University Press.

Heckman, James J. and James M. Snyder. 1997. Linear Probability Models of the Demand for Attributes with an Empirical Application to Estimating the Preferences of Legislators. *The Rand Journal of Economics* 28(0) Special Issue: S142–89.

Hibbs, Douglas A. 1977. Political Parties and Macroeconomic Policy. *American Political Science Review* 71: 1467–87.

Horn, Murray J. 1995. *The Political Economy of Public Administration: Institutional Choice in the Public Sector.* Cambridge: Cambridge University Press.

Bibliography

Hsiao, Cheng. 1986. *Analysis of Panel Data.* Cambridge: Cambridge University Press.

International Monetary Fund. *International Financial Statistics.* International Monetary Fund: Washington, DC, various years.

Jones, David M. 1995. *The Buck Starts Here.* Englewood Cliffs, NJ: Prentice Hall.

Kane, Edward J. 1974. The Re-politicization of the Fed. *Journal of Financial and Quantitative Analysis* 9: 743–52.

Kane, Edward J. 1975. New Congressional Restraints and Federal Reserve Independence. *Challenge* 18: 37–44.

Kane, Edward J. 1980. Politics and Fed Policymaking: The More Things Change the More They Remain the Same. *Journal of Monetary Economics* 6: 199–211.

Keech, William R. and Irwin L. Morris. 1996. Appointments, Presidential Power, and the Federal Reserve. *Journal of Macroeconomics* 19(2): 253–67.

Kenen, Peter B. 1995. *Economic and Monetary Union in Europe.* New York: Cambridge University Press.

Keohane, Robert. 1984. *After Hegemony.* Princeton: Princeton University Press.

Kettl, Donald F. 1986. *Leadership at the Fed.* New Haven: Yale University Press.

Khoury, Salwa S. 1990. The Federal Reserve Reaction Function: A Specification Search. In *The Political Economy of American Monetary Policy*, Thomas Mayer, ed. Cambridge: Cambridge University Press.

Kolko, Gabriel. 1967. *Triumph of Conservatism: A Reinterpretation of American History 1900–1916.* Chicago: Quadrangle Books.

Kosters, Wim, Manfred J. M. Neumann, Renate Ohr, Roland Vaubel, et al. 1998. German Economics Professors Convinced 'Orderly Postponement' of Euro Essential. Letters to the Editor. *Financial Times* February 9, 1998.

Krause, George A. 1994. Federal Reserve Policy Decision Making: Political and Bureaucratic Influences. *American Journal of Political Science* 38(1): 124–44.

Krehbiel, Keith. 1990. Are Congressional Committees Composed of Preference Outliers? *American Political Science Review* 84(1): 149–63.

Krehbiel, Keith and Douglas Rivers. 1988. The Analysis of Committee Power: An Application to Senate Voting on the Minimum Wage. *American Journal of Political Science* 32(4): 1151–74.

Kreps, David M. 1990. *A Course in Microeconomic Theory.* Princeton: Princeton University Press.

Kydland, Finn E. and Edward C. Prescott. 1977. Rules Rather Than Discretion: The Inconsistency of Optimal Plans. *Journal of Political Economy* 85: 473–92.

Lemieux, Peter H. and Charles H. Stewart III. 1990. Senate Confirmation of Supreme Court Nominations from Washington to Reagan. *Working Papers in Political Science* P-90-3. The Hoover Institution, Stanford University.

Livingston, James. 1986. *Origins of the Federal Reserve System: Money, Class and Corporate Capitalism 1890–1913.* Ithaca, NY: Cornell University Press.

Lohmann, Susanne. 1992. Optimal Credibility in Monetary Policy: Credibility versus Flexibility. *American Economic Review* 82: 273–86.

Lohmann, Susanne. 1997. Partisan Control of the Money Supply and Decentralized Appointment Powers. *European Journal of Political Economy* 13: 225–46.

Lombra, Raymond E. and Nicholas Karamouzis. 1990. A Positive Analysis of the Policy-Making Process at the Federal Reserve. In *Political Economy of American*

Monetary Policy, Thomas Mayer, ed. Cambridge: Cambridge University Press.

Mackenzie, G. Calvin. 1981. *The Politics of Presidential Appointments*. New York: Free Press.

Maisel, Sherman. 1973. *Managing the Dollar*. New York: Norton.

Martin, Justin. 2000. Greenspan: *The Man Behind Money*. Cambridge, MA: Perseus.

Matthews, Steven A. 1989. Veto Threat: Rhetoric in a Bargaining Game. *Quarterly Journal of Economics* 104: 347–69.

Mayer, Thomas. 1990. *The Political Economy of American Monetary Policy*. Cambridge: Cambridge University Press.

McCarty, Nolan M. 1997. Presidential Reputation and the Veto. *Economics and Politics* 9(1): 1–26.

McCarty, Nolan M. and Keith T. Poole. 1995. Veto Power and Legislation: An Empirical Analysis of Executive and Legislative Bargaining from 1961 to 1986. *Journal of Law, Economics and Organization* 11(2): 282–312.

McCarty, Nolan M. and Rose Razaghian. 1999. Advice and Consent: Senate Responses to Executive Branch Nominations 1885–1996. *American Journal of Political Science* 43(3): 1122–43.

McCubbins, Mathew D. and Thomas Schwartz. 1984. Oversight Overlooked: Police Patrols vs. Fire Alarms. *American Journal of Political Science* 28: 165–79.

McCubbins, Mathew D., Roger G. Noll, and Barry R. Weingast. 1987. Administrative Procedures as Instruments of Political Control. *Journal of Law, Economics, and Organization* 3: 243–77.

Milgrom, Paul and John Roberts. 1992. *Economics, Organization and Management*. Englewood Cliffs, NJ: Prentice-Hall.

Moe, Terry. 1984. The New Economics of Organization. *American Journal of Political Science* 28: 739–77.

Moe, Terry. 1985. Control and Feedback in Economic Regulation: The Case of the NLRB. *The American Political Science Review* 79: 1094–116.

Moe, Terry. 1987a. An Assessment of the Positive Theory of Congressional Dominance. *Legislative Studies Quarterly* 12: 472–520.

Moe, Terry. 1987b. Interests, Institutions, and Positive Theory: The Politics of the NLRB. *Studies in American Policy Development* 2: 236–99.

Moe, Terry. 1989. The Politics of Bureaucratic Structure. In *Can the Government Govern?*, John Chubb and Paul Peterson, eds. Washington, D.C.: Brookings Institution.

Moe, Terry. 1991. Politics and the Theory of Organization. *Journal of Law, Economics, and Organization* 7: 106–29.

Moraski, Bryon and Charles Shipan. 1999. The Politics of Supreme Court Nominations: A Theory of Institutional Constraints and Choices. *American Journal of Political Science*. Forthcoming.

Morris, Irwin L. 1991. Appointment Power. Federal Reserve Governors, and Monetary Policy: On the Trail of Presidential Influence. M.A. Thesis: Political Science. University of North Carolina, Chapel Hill.

Morris, Irwin L. 1994. Congress, the President, and the Federal Reserve: The Politics of American Monetary Policy. Ph.D. Thesis: Political Science. University of North Carolina, Chapel Hill.

Morris, Irwin L. 2000. Congress, the President, and the Federal Reserve: The Politics of American Monetary Policy-Making. Ann Arbor, The University of Michigan Press.

Morris, Irwin L. and Michael Munger. 1997. First Branch, or Root? The Congress, the President, and the Federal Reserve. *Public Choice* 96(3–4): 363–80.

Moser, Peter. 1997. Checks and Balances, and the Supply of Central Bank Independence. Unpublished working paper. University of St. Gallen, St. Gallen, Switzerland.

Mundell, Robert A. 1961. A Theory of Optimum Currency Areas. *American Economic Review* 51: 657–65.

Niskanen, William. 1971. *Bureaucracy and Representative Government*. Chicago: Aldineo Atherton.

Nokken, Timothy P. and Brian R. Sala. 2000. Confirmation Dynamics: A Model of Presidential Appointments to Independent Agencies. *Journal of Theoretical Politics* 12: 91–112.

Nordhaus, William D. 1975. The Political Business Cycle. *Review of Economic Studies* 42: 169–90.

North, Douglass C. and Barry R. Weingast. 1989. Constitutions and Commitment: Evolution of Institutions Governing Public Choice. *Journal of Economic History* 49(4): 803–32.

Olson, Mancur. 1965. *The Logic of Collective Action: Public Goods and the Theory of Groups*. Cambridge, MA: Harvard University Press.

Organization for Economic Co-operation and Development (OECD). 1997. *OECD Economic Outlook* vol. 61: June.

Peltzman, Sam. 1976. Toward a More General Theory of Regulation. *Journal of Law and Economics* 19(2): 211–347.

Persson, Torsten and Guido Tabellini. 1990. *Macroeconomic Policy, Credibility, and Politics*. London: Harwood Academic Publishers.

Persson, Torsten and Guido Tabellini, eds. 1994. *Monetary and Fiscal Policy. Volume 1: Credibility*. Boston: MIT Press.

Persson, Torsten and Guido Tabellini. 1999. Political Economics and Macroeconomic Policy. In *The Handbook of Macroeconomics*, John B. Taylor and Michael Woodford, eds. Oxford: Elsevier Science, North-Holland.

Pierce, James. 1978. The Myth of Congressional Supervision of Monetary Policy. *Journal of Monetary Economics* 4: 363–70.

Poole, Keith T. and Howard Rosenthal. 1985. A Spatial Model for Legislative Roll Call Analysis. *American Journal of Political Science* 29: 357–84.

Poole, Keith T. and Howard Rosenthal. 1997. *Congress: A Political-Economic History of Roll Call Voting*. NY: Oxford University Press.

Puckett, Richard. 1984. Federal Open Market Committee Structure. *Journal of Monetary Economics* 12: 97–104.

Reagan, Michael D. 1961. The Political Structure of the Federal Reserve System. *American Political Science Review* 55: 81–103.

Reserve Bank Act of Australia. 1959.

Roche, David. 1996. Europe's Faded Photocopy Democracy. *Euromoney* December: 24–5.

Rogoff, Kenneth. 1985. The Optimal Degree of Commitment to an Intermediate Target. *Quarterly Journal of Economics* 100: 1169–90.

Rogoff, Kenneth. 1990. Equilibrium Political Budget Cycles. *American Economic Review* 80: 21–36.

Rogoff, Kenneth and Anne Sibert. 1988. Elections and Macroeconomic Policy Cycles. *Review of Economic Studies* 55: 1–16.

Romer, Thomas and Howard Rosenthal. 1978. Political Resource Allocation, Controlled Agendas, and the Status Quo. *Public Choice* 33: 27–44.

Rose, Sanford. 1974. The Agony of the Fed. *Fortune* 90: 90–3, 180–90.

Rubinstein, Ariel. 1982. Perfect Equilibrium in a Bargaining Model. *Econometrica* 50: 97–109.

Schaling, Eric. 1995. *Institutions and Monetary Policy: Credibility, Flexibility and Central Bank Independence*. Aldershots, Hants, UK: Edward Elgar.

Scheffe, Henry. 1959. *The Analysis of Variance*. NY: John Wiley and Sons, Inc.

Segal, Jeffrey A., Charles M. Cameron, and Albert D. Cover. 1992. A Spatial Model of Roll Call Voting: Senators, Constituents, Presidents, and Interest Groups in Supreme Court Confirmations. *American Journal of Political Science* 36(1): 96–121.

Senate Committee on Banking, Housing and Urban Affairs. 1975. *Monetary Policy Oversight* February 25.

Senate Committee on Banking, Housing and Urban Affairs. 1975–6. *First through Fourth Meetings on the Conduct of Monetary Policy, House Concurrent Resolution 133*.

Senate Committee on Banking, Housing and Urban Affairs. 1977–8. *First through Third Meetings on the Conduct of Monetary Policy, House Concurrent Resolution 133 and Public Law 95–188*.

Senate Committee on Banking, Housing and Urban Affairs. 1979–95. *Federal Reserve's [First or Second] Monetary Policy Report for [Year], Full Employment and Balanced Growth Act of 1978 (Humphrey-Hawkins), Semiannual hearings*. February and July of each year.

Senate Committee on Banking, Housing and Urban Affairs, Subcommittee on Production and Stabilization. 1974. *Oversight on Economic Stabilization* February 6.

Snyder, Susan, and Barry Weingast. 2000. The American System of Shared Powers: The President, Congress, and the NLRB. *Journal of Law, Economics, and Organization* 16: 269–305.

Stigler, George. 1971. The Theory of Economic Regulation. *Bell Journal of Economics and Management Science* 2: 3–21.

Taylor, John. 1993. Discretion versus Policy Rules in Practice. *Carnegie-Rochester Conference Series on Public Policy* 39: 195–214.

Taylor, John B. and Michael Woodford, eds. 1999. *The Handbook of Macroeconomics*. Oxford: Elsevier Science, North-Holland.

Bibliography

Timberlake, Richard H. 1993. *Monetary Policy in the United States*. Chicago: University of Chicago Press.

Treaty on European Union. 1992.

Tufte, Edward R. 1975. Determinants of the Outcomes of Midterm Congressional Elections. *American Political Science Review* 69: 812–26.

U.S. Department of Commerce Bureau of Economic Analysis. *Business Cycle Indicators*.

U.S. Department of Commerce Bureau of Economic Analysis. *Business Statistics*.

Waller, Christopher J. 1992. A Bargaining Model of Partisan Appointments to the Central Bank. *Journal of Monetary Economics* 29(3): 411–28.

Waller, Christopher J. and Carl E. Walsh. 1996. Central-Bank Independence, Economic Behavior, and Optimal Term Lengths. *American Economic Review* 86(5): 1139–53.

Weingast, Barry R. 1984. The Congressional-Bureaucratic System: A Principal-Agent Perspective (with applications to the SEC). *Public Choice* 44: 147–92.

Weingast, Barry R. and William J. Marshall. 1988. The Industrial Organization of Congress; or, Why Legislatures, Like Firms, Are Not Organized as Markets. *Journal of Political Economy* 96(1): 132–63.

Weingast, Barry R. and William J. Marshall. 1989. Regulation and the Theory of Legislative Choice: The Interstate Commerce Act of 1887. *Journal of Law and Economics* XXXII: 35–61.

Weingast, Barry R. and Mark J. Moran. 1983. Bureaucratic Discretion or Congressional Control? Regulatory Policymaking by the Federal Trade Commission. *Journal of Political Economy* 91: 765–800.

Wessel, David. 1996. Rohatyn Considered for No. 2 Fed Post. *Wall Street Journal* January 19, 1996: A2, A5.

Wessel, David. 1997. Fed Funds Rate Left Unchanged One More Time. *Wall Street Journal* October 1, 1997: A2, A10.

West, Robert C. 1977. *Banking Reform and the Federal Reserve: 1863–1923*. London: Cornell University.

White, Eugene Nelson. 1983. *The Regulation and Reform of the American Banking System, 1900–1929*. Princeton: Princeton University Press.

Whittlesey, C. R. 1963. Power and Influence in the Federal Reserve System. *Economica* 45: 123–35.

Wiebe, Robert H. 1962. *Businessmen and Reform: A Study of the Progressive Movement*. Cambridge, MA: Harvard.

Wilke, John R. 1996a. Clinton Names Greenspan to New Term At the Fed, Rivlin and Meyer to Its Board. *Wall Street Journal* February 23, 1996: A3.

Wilke, John R. 1996b. Rohatyn Pulls Out of Consideration for Fed Post. *Wall Street Journal* February 14, 1996: A2.

Wilke, John R. 1996c. Clinton Lists His Choices for Fed Seats. *Wall Street Journal* February 20, 1996: A3.

Wilke, John R. and Michael K. Frisby. 1996. GOP Shakes Hopes to Name Rohatyn to Fed. *Wall Street Journal* February 13, 1996: A3, A16.

Williamson, Oliver E. 1975. *Markets and Hierarchies*. New York: Free Press.

Williamson, Oliver E. 1981. The Economics of Organization: The Transaction Cost Approach. *American Journal of Sociology* 87(3): 547–77.

Bibliography

Woolley, John T. 1984. *The Federal Reserve and the Politics of Monetary Policy.* Cambridge: Cambridge University Press.

Yohe, William P. 1966. A Study of Federal Open Market Committee Voting 1955–64. *Southern Economic Journal* 12: 98–117.

Zupan, Mark A. 1992. Measuring the Ideological Preferences of U.S. Presidents: A Proposed (Extremely Simple) Method. *Public Choice* 73: 351–61.

Index

Other Books in the Series (*continued from page iii*)